AN ANGLER AT LARGE

BY

WILLIAM ÇAINE

(W. QUILLIAM *of the* "*Field*")

WITH A FRONTISPIECE IN COLOUR FROM A DRAWING
BY GEORGE SHERINGHAM

LONDON
KEGAN PAUL, TRENCH, TRÜBNER & CO. L^{TD}
DRYDEN HOUSE, GERRARD STREET, W.
1911

DEDICATORY LETTER

DEAR H. T. S.,
   It is a commonplace that there are too
many books on angling.

My instinct, therefore, is to follow the established
custom of authors who write on that subject, and
hypocritically to apologise for what I have done.

But gratitude compels me to dedicate the
Angler at Large to you, the man the most truly,
though perhaps not the most conspicuously, responsible for its appearance. For lacking your
encouragements (of which this book is the most
direct fruit), very possibly I had been still flounder-
ing clueless in the labyrinth of Conveyancing Law,
and employing my pen upon the infinitely dis-
creditable labour of storing up trouble for the
harmless unborn children of inoffensive clients.
You have done more than any twenty men
(though less than one woman) to save me from
this misery and infamy, and I hold myself bound
publicly to testify my obligation.

You are, then, the natural dedicatee of this book.

But if I follow the custom which I have mentioned—if, that is to say, I apologise for adding to

our prodigious list of Angling books, what kind of a compliment do I pay you, upon whom responsibility must so seriously fall? I should be slighting your taste most villainously.

I decline, therefore, to follow that custom. I do not apologise for the *Angler at Large*. I prefer to say that the book is a good book, and that I congratulate the public on its appearance. I do not hesitate to own that it is a book which I am glad to possess; that I am sure it is one which a great number of people ought to buy—if only to give it instantly away. I will even declare that it is a book which should be translated into all polite languages.

I could develop this theme indefinitely, but I find that, while I am putting its proper valuation upon your judgment, I am almost losing sight of that modesty which it still behoves an author in some degree to preserve.

I think enough has been said to show that I am in a very embarrassing situation.

So here is the book for you.

Always yours,
WILLIAM CAINE.

HAMPSTEAD, 1911.

NOTE

I THANK the proprietors of the *Field*, *Macmillan's Magazine*, and the *Evening Standard and St. James's Gazette* for their permission to use, in this book, articles which they have published. Those from the *Field* were originally entitled: The Friendship of the River, A Day with the Keeper, Some Dry-fly Refinements, A Blank Day, The Great Dry-fly Myth, The Purism of Flounder Fishing, The Crackling of Thorns, Fishing Trophies, The Patience of Anglers, The Perfect Thrill, The Trout at the Boundary, Then and Now, The Essential Falsity, Three Days on the Sea-Stream, and A Norwegian Interlude.

To *Macmillan's Magazine* I am indebted for Isaac on a Chalk Stream, and to the *Evening Standard and St. James's Gazette* for Mors Janua, in this book called Of Death.

CONTENTS

AN ANGLER AT LARGE

I

OF US, A HARP AND A SPANISH JUG

AS the Valley began to open out my head was always at one window or the other. Because of the luggage the fly was a closed one. It is sinful to drive to Willows in a closed thing, but what would you? To say nothing of the rain, unless people are bound for one of those eccentric restorative establishments in Germany where nudity is compulsory, a few boxes are bound to accompany their migration.

So we had with us:

1. A harp in a harp-case.
2. An American trunk, not quite so large as a Pantechnicon van.
3. A steamer trunk, not quite so large as the last.
4. A telescopic basket.
5. Another telescopic basket.
6. Another telescopic basket.

B

7. A sausage of green rot-proof canvas.
8. A handbag.
9. A tea-basket (called Grandmama).
10. A fishing-creel.
11. A bundle of fishing-rods and other engines.
12. A roll of rugs.
13. A Rookee chair, in a bag of canvas (rot-proof).

All this crammed to bursting-point.

But no canary and no bicycle. Nor any dog.

Numbers 4 to 13 incommoded us within, or crowded the roof and the box seat. Numbers 2 and 3 travelled behind us in a luggage cart. The harp, in the harp-case, closed the procession on a milk-float.

Few people travel with a harp. This accounts for the prosperity of Mr. Cook, Dr. Lunn and other convenient gentlemen. ·

Harps are provided in Heaven. Otherwise there would be no orchestra.

The cost of appeasing porters when travelling with one of these instruments explains the dimensions of the Hebrew variety. This is an unworthy sneer at an admirable race. It is the fault of the harp. I am at my worst just after the thing has accompanied me on a journey. To-morrow it will be taken out and strung up and played, and then I shall love it again. In this—in nothing else—it resembles a young child, which, when it has been washed and fed and has slept and has been washed and fed once more, becomes something adorable and entirely different from the curse of yesterday's railway travel.

The harp-case has power to turn smiling, kindly, bearded men into brutal Grobians. They fetch out the trunks with a jest; whistling, load their barrows with sausages and telescopic baskets. "Anything more, sir?" they ask alertly. "There is only," I reply, with my forced smile, "a harp." And the weather changes for the worse. Two, three, four of them bend their enormous muscles to the toil. I see their honest faces redden, grow purple. I hear muttered words which I recognise as popular expressions of hate. While elevating their outrageous fardel to the roof of our conveyance they give themselves permanent strains. They rupture their abdominal walls. They become out-patients at infirmaries and bind themselves in trusses. They lose their situations. Their children starve. Their sticks are sold up. At least, I imagine all these things happening.

And to change these sour-faced, fainting, loathing, blasphemous enemies back into friends, what sums are needful!

I do not mind the loss of money—the harp is ready for the road—but the thought of these

men's animosity is very painful to me.   For I
would go about the world among smiles and kind
words.   A humble ambition, but not easy to
realise.

To-day, however, the business was not so dire
as usual.   The proprietor of our cottage had sent
his milk-float to meet us.   Strange prompting of
Providence !   A milk-float is low, near the earth.
You can slide things from a barrow into a milk-
float.   It is, therefore, the most suitable conveyance imaginable for harps that have arrived at
railway stations.   The transfer was effected without a suspicion of hernia.   But the milk-float was
full.   Yet—astonishing and mysterious Destiny !
—the proprietor of the fly, which I had ordered,
had sent also a luggage cart.   Thus, owing to our
farmer-landlord having provided what must have
seemed to him twice the accommodation necessary
for our baggage, and to the fly's proprietor
(undesired) having furnished a cart which he
had, no doubt, thought of quite a reasonable size,
we were able, by careful packing of all three
vehicles, to get ourselves and our indispensables
carried in one journey to our and their destination.

This kind of thing is largely responsible for the
widespread belief that Providence is a good person
to leave things to.   Occasionally Providence, when

it is left to him, turns up trumps.   These things remain fixed in our memories and obliterate the recollection of those innumerable opportunities which we have afforded to Providence of which no heed has been taken.

I myself leave things to Providence, but not from any confidence I possess in Providence.   I think he is a very bad man to leave things to. Quite rightly he does not encourage that sort of thing at all.

But it is less trouble than seeing to things oneself.   It is time enough for that when one has to.

Sometimes, moreover, it comes off.   And then it is delightful.

And in the case of the harp and the milk-float, remember, I had not left it to Providence at all. In my mind I had provided a railway van for everything.   Yes, I was going to send everything out in a railway van.   And no railway van would have been available, because the railway tells me that it does not send vans outside the city boundaries.   But Providence saw to the matter, and sent me a milk-float and a luggage cart, which was positively noble of Providence.

With this good omen we drove away from the station, and presently the Valley began to open out, and my head began to travel between the windows.

There was Ottley Down on the right. By springing across the fly I was just in time to see the chimneys of Little Ottley House, and, to their left, the White Poplars at the lower end of the water. Here the horse's head got in my way, and in order to catch my first glimpse of the Little Ottley Chalk Pit, I had to tread once more upon my wife's feet, only as they were by this time curled up on the seat beside her, I didn't. In taking my head in from viewing the chalk-pit, so that I might get over to where I could obtain a sight of the Hanging Wood, I knocked my hat off into the mud and the fly had to halt. I recovered my hat, sadly bewrayed, and as I climbed in, "Never mind," said I to my wife, "I won't want it for three months, thank Heaven!" With these words I sat down on the Spanish Jug.

This utensil should have been mentioned in my list. But it is too late now. I give it a place to itself.

14. A Spanish Jug.

The history of the Spanish Jug.

In the Spring of this present year my wife told me that I wished to write a novel whose theatre should be Spain. I was very glad to hear this, because I knew how much she desired to visit that country.

After an interval we were in Madrid.

Next day my wife observed a woman carrying a large earthen jug, twin-spouted, of elegant shape. My wife coveted it. After that she saw nothing but women carrying similar jugs.

Presently I began to feel an influence akin to that experienced by the hypnotic subject. I became aware of a consciousness that I desired one of these jugs. I knew that I did not really want a jug of any kind, because I dislike all jugs. But from time to time I found myself saying, in reply to a question, "Yes, we must certainly take one of those jugs home," or, "Yes, it would look well upon Victoria" (which is the name of our sideboard), or, "Yes, it would be the very thing to keep water in during the hot days." After a week of this I found myself bartering coppers against a Spanish Jug, this very one upon which I sat when I got back into the fly. It was, it is, an enormous jug.

"It is fragile," I said, as I lugged the thing back through Madrid. "And it is too large for the bag. It will only get broken on the journey. Let us give it away to somebody and increase our popularity."

"I will take it to England," said my wife, "if I carry it every step of the way." This emphatic manner of speaking (for we were to travel by train and steamboat) convinced me that what she promised would happen in every particular but one, an important one.

During the journey to London my wife comforted me, whenever I complained of the Spanish Jug's excessive weight, by drawing word-pictures of Victoria adorned with the Spanish Jug and prophesying about the great draughts of cold water which I should, during the hot days, quaff from the Spanish Jug. She said that she would never have let me burden us with the jug if I had not been so mad about it in Madrid, if I had not persuaded her, with all that about Victoria and the coldness of water kept in such jugs, to let me buy it. So, mindful of my past enthusiasm, I, sweating, carried it through innumerable railway stations and customs-houses into steamboats and omnibuses and cabs and restaurants and railway carriages and buffets. For it was too fragile for a porter's clumsy hands.

At last I sat upon it, as I have told. But I did not crush it. It was not fragile enough for that.

Suppose I finish with the Spanish Jug now and for ever. Let me advance this narrative about twenty minutes.

While the harp and the harp-case were earning me the undying hatred of the flyman, the driver of the luggage cart, the driver of the milk-float, and the gardener at our cottage, I, passing through the dining-room, a prey to agitated thoughts, discovered my wife in the act of filling the Spanish Jug with water from a glass vessel of common shape.

"There!" she said, standing back and surveying it fondly, "now *wasn't* it worth a little trouble? It will always stand here"—and she set it on a shelf—"filled, so that you will have sweet, cold water to drink whenever you want it. And there is a glass to stand beside it." With these words she hurried off to her bedroom to unpack the American trunk.

Ten minutes later, having done my best to allay the detestation of four fellow-creatures, I returned to the dining-room. I was hot and tired. For it was not only by money that I had curried favour with those men. I had helped with the harp-case. I was, I say, hot and tired.

My eye fell upon the Spanish Jug and its attendant glass.

The words "sweet, cold water" recurred to me.

I possessed myself of the Spanish Jug.

I tilted it above its glass.

Nothing happened. I said: "The nozzle is blocked up."

I blew into the nozzle.

A sound resembling the hollow roar of the wind in a sea-cave resulted.

Then I perceived that my hands were wet.

Then I discovered that I was standing in a large pool of water.

Then I knew that the Spanish Jug leaked.

And a great cry broke from me in my agony.

My wife appeared, pallid. "Your jug leaks," I said.

"Tut!" said she, "so it does. What a mess! Well," she rang the bell for sponges and cloths, "it will still look nice on Victoria. And after all that was really what made you buy it."

To resume my broken thread.

All these things—the chimney of Little Ottley, the Hanging Wood, the Island Willows, the Green Man (Dwarf it should be, so small is this public-house) and the rest—I found in their places. Each discovery filled me with greater and greater content. Nothing was altered. The Valley was just as I had known it, not a hedge gone, not a gate added, not a—Hold! What is this along the top of Lavender's garden wall? Gods and great Humphrey! Corrugated iron. Oh, John Lavender, John Lavender! Is there never a thatcher left in Clere Vale to save thee from this villainy? Oh, damned utilitarian! Oh, Vandal Lavender! Oh! Oh! and again Oh! Drive fast, good flyman, or I shall be writing in praise of thatch on walls of yellow mud, and never get to the cottage to-night.

Let me ignore the presence of the machine-made horror. Let me feast my eyes rather on the brave, new, golden roof with which, Lavender, thou hast positively bought thy pardon. Bravo! A good roof; a haystack house. Excellent John! Thou knowest the merits of the material, cool in hot weather, warm in cold. For its beauty thou givest not a curse. No matter. Pass the wall. The sweet stuff is thick on thy house, and I am obliged to thee and to all good fellows who keep up the thatching trade.

And there is our own roof. What a roof it is! Old thatch mended. You cannot find a brown or a yellow that is not in it. And the tilt of it! And its amplitude! It sits on the house like a cosy on a teapot. Let the sun burn or the wind blow frozen, neither shall find his way through that. It is the only stuff to shelter agriculturists. For to each his appropriate roofing. Slate for the trader, hard, cold, mathematical. And tiles, which are only glorified slates, they are well for the retired soldiers at Eastbourne, who are a cut above business. But for the tiller of the soil, from the soil let his roof be won. For this agriculture is the completest of arts, and can give a man every necessary thing, food, bedding, beer, wool for his back, sport for his leisure, and the house from chimney to cellar.

His daughter's piano ? Why, this is the first time I ever heard his daughter's piano numbered among a man's necessities.

Am I an agriculturist? God forbid! I am a man writing for money, and now I have written about thatch and we are at the gate, and the harp, in the harp-case, has to be got into the drawing-room.

II

OF THE FRIENDSHIP OF THE RIVER

I AM going to fish.

It is true that there is an enormous deal to be done in the house. The unpacking of the American trunk is in itself a day's work. And there is the drawing-room furniture to rearrange.

Wherever we go—and you must know that we are always going somewhere—this ceremony begins our sojourn, because, as my wife would tell you, I have my particular views upon the placing of tables and chairs and the Oriental fabrics which brighten up the dingiest room. I like to see what is called 'the feminine touch' in my habitation. What is good enough for careless bachelors is not good enough, believe her, for me. I can never do anything until I have got the harp out of the harp-case and the harp-case into the back premises out of sight—ugly thing! And if there is no sofa, I will carry a bed down from an upper room and cover it with djidjims and cushions and feign a divan, rather than allow my drawing-room to lack

13

this essentially feminine touch. And when my wife is on it, then and not till then do I feel that the place begins to be habitable. Ask her if this is not so.

And I will work far into the night, long after she has grown exhausted, carrying out her excellent suggestions, lugging great wardrobes across and across the floor till they are in exactly the situation to make right the new adjustment of the large tables and the piano, if there is one.

And I welcome every suggestion she makes (from the couch that used to be a bed), because I know her to have a sound instinct for placing furniture. It is extraordinary how sound it is. We always agree—in the end. How lucky it is that we should be married! Supposing she had wedded a man who detested this kind of hard labour. An unfastidious man. A man such as I used to be before I knew her.

Just now, however, I am going to fish.

The harp I will unpack and the harp-case I will help the gardener to carry away. And I will swab up the leakage of the Spanish Jug, and then I will fish.

For you are to know, sir, that I have not fished in chalk water these three years. It is absolutely necessary for me to angle.

And you are also to know, sir—(No, my wife,

no. No tea. Well, a cup—while I get on my
waders and put the rod together). You are also,
sir, to know that it is six years since I said good-
bye to this same river Clere, my companion of
five summers. How then shall I shift furniture
or empty trunks, when he is all agog to greet
me?

Come, let us be off. Will you go with me?
The lady of the house is busy, and I am happy
and prepared to prattle.

I say, sir, that we grow into friendship with a
long-fished river as with a good comrade. The
odd days, never repeated, that we have had on
other waters are comparable to those single, rare,
glorious encounters with the choice spirits, which
Circumstance forbids us to improve. At the
dinner-table, in a railway train, yea, by the water's
edge we meet. Heart goes out to heart; each
recognises in the other something of himself. It
is a moment pregnant with the excitement of discovery, with all the possibilities that congeniality
offers. One thinks, "If I were not going to
Australia to-morrow!"; the other, "Would this
man awaited me in Archangel! I could love him
like a brother." Yet, though we never meet
again, we remember, not perhaps the name, not
perhaps the features, but something which is
independent of these accidents. Friendship is

largely a matter of opportunity. That one memory is all the friendship opportunity allows us. So with these rivers of a single day.

But when one has fished a water season after season for five years, then is its friendship a great and living thing. Of that little burn in Mull where one made such hay of the sea-trout one cherishes but a dim picture of dark pools, miniature brown-white cataracts, slate-blue hills, a leaden sky, the calling of the moor-fowl, and a heavy basket. But each feature of the long-fished stream is with one at all times—each curve and vista, each willow and withy-bed, the unguessable hatch-hole, the frank, revealing shallow, and the swelling downs and the distant clumps. These things are a possession that nothing can destroy so long as memory serves. Though paralysis should strike one into a living death, while memory were faithful one should yet wander in one's mind (by no means deliriously) through certain green water-meadows, eye busy with a certain stream where stout fish should always be rising. Other friends, older perhaps, dearer even than the river, should stand by the bedside, grieving at one's insensibility to their presence. Blind, deaf, dumb, feeling nothing, how should one cry to them for comfort? And what comfort could they give? But the river would come at one's unspoken call, and its consolation would never fail.

The winter months and all other times when trout fishing is impossible are in a sense seasons of paralysis.   One may be rather more independent of one's river friend than one would be in the unfortunate circumstances which I have just imagined; but, though others claim one's attention, excluding him from one's communication, he bears no malice.   He never sulks, thinking himself slighted.   If a common friend happens to engage one's attention, and the presence of the river is suggested, he will come cheerfully to make a third, stay as long as the others wish, promoting pleasant talk with all his might, and, at a hint, will fade unostentatiously away.   He knows nothing of jealousy, nothing of priorities; he is humble, faithful, always cheerful, always fresh, always the most excellent of company.   And one never dreams of despising him for his lack of spirit, which one would surely do—such is man—were he a human being.   He is like a dog, without its sycophancy; like a pipe, without its perversity; like the supreme book, without its——He is like the supreme book.   Yet the supreme book demands physical effort.   Eyes tire even of the supreme book.   And the supreme book, too,

c

is shut into outer darkness by paralysis. To an angler the river beloved is really like nothing else.

And when he is by—when, that is, we are by by him—what good times we have! How we vary the sport! His population, I have said, is always rising. Each of those dimples is made by a fish that one has risen, played, and landed. And — this is the peculiar advantage of the situation—always those fishes are ready to be risen, played, and landed again. No day, not even memory's, is long enough to grass the fishes of five seasons. So one picks and one chooses, taking one here, one there, passing others by, reserving them for other occasions. They will not desert their places.

Does our pleasure demand a rise of Mayfly? What fishing we can cram into a couple of hours! Thirty trout, and the balance dips to 70 lb. And we might have done still better, but this is enough for good sportsmen such as we and the river are. Or do we feel that a clear October day would be well spent among the grayling? It is at our service. The woods are bravely decked out in honour of the occasion. The sun is warm; the air is cold. The fish rise foolishly, and our take is colossal. Especially in the long deeps of the Still Reach do the great head-and-tailers break the

surface.   How they tug and bore!   What
lengths of the bank we cover and cover as we
follow those mighty fishes down the water to
net them at last where the deep thins to the
broad, gravelly shallow!   Or is our fancy for
some particular fish, that yellow monster that
we got on the half-volley at our very feet as he
came sulkily down to us, scared by the fish that
we had pricked, the mighty trout that was looking
into our eye as we flung the badger hackle at him,
the golden giant that we hoped only to hasten,
the colossus that we could hardly get into the
net—the greatest trout?   Do we care to live
again through the marvellous moment of his
rising?   It is just as we please.   Or there is
the big fellow in the shallow, jungly backwater,
that ran straight into a little patch of weed (a
willow just above, an ash just below), and the rod
being stoutly held up, splashed his way to the top,
and so lay on his side, his head out of water, and
taught us a new wrinkle for managing a weeded fish
by holding him thus until he expires of asphyxia-
tion.   What though the wrinkle has never been
used again?   What though the odds against the
possibility of its employment are 20,000 to 1?
Let us warm ourselves in the glow of our own
self-esteem, that we were able to realise the master-
liness of inactivity, and so, ultimately, wade in and

net a $2\frac{1}{2}$ pounder, after one rush of six yards and three minutes of holding on. What though, conscience-stricken, we turned him in again? We had him. Let us have him again. Let us turn him in once more, and good luck go with him, slowly, under the willow roots.

Or would we have a few fat brace with the sedge? The feast is spread. We have only to name our dish. Our good friend will see that we are provided. He can meet our every taste. For an epicurean meal of choice morsels, for a great lusty gourmandising, he has the ingredients ready to hand, and his kindly presence will add savour to every mouthful.

Seasons come, perhaps, when we cannot actually meet. Our occasions take us elsewhere. But we are not utterly separated from the river. At any moment we have only to shut our eyes to be on his banks, catching fish. And then our circumstances smile. We are reunited. And as we cross the lowest meadow to where, deep and calm under the protecting copse, our friend awaits us by the boundary fence (there is surely a great trout under the thorn bush), we catch a kindly wink from him far up where he turns westward, and our heart beats its answer to his welcome.

And there he is.

   .   .   .   .   .   .

I am going to fish.   Now,—at once,—I am going to fish.

III

OF TO-NIGHT

TO-NIGHT the garden was delicious. The sky was covered with a film of cloud which diffused the light of the moon (in her first quarter) all over the heavens into a soft and radiant blue. She hung just above the greatest of that row of elms which burdens the western sky line. A high branch touched her. The big trees loomed imminent, rather terrible. The great one seemed to crouch there, huge, devilish. In two clear places among its branches there seemed the long slit eyes in the head of a bushy and shapeless demon. It must have been the immense and contrasting peace of the night that put this gruesome idea into my head. The elm-fiend was to the rest of my circumstances like that abominable anticipation of trouble which so often does its best to kill complete happiness. Low among the arms of the smaller, thinner elms to the south, lightning flickered, just above the down. The stars shone very faint, largely luminous. A sigh of breeze stirred rarely. Sounds are never absent in the

country, whose silence is made up of a multitude
of little noises. Distinct above the rest was the
coo of a pigeon from the clump on the flank of
the Beacon Down. A cow mooed. The starlings
rustled in the thatch above our heads. Somewhere a nightjar sprung its stealthy rattle, and
a river bird called once. And four miles away
at the station the trains whistled and rolled and
puffed, the sound coming loud, caught by the
funnel which is this valley, across whose mouth
from N.E. to S.W. the railway line runs. Let it
run!

And the air, dear God! it seemed to fill one's
whole body. We could not drink enough of it.

This is a good place. It always was. But it is
better now.

IV

OF THE OTHER RODS, AND PARTICULARLY
OF MR. BLENNERHASSETT

JOE tells me that this season there are three men besides myself who are entitled to fish hereabouts.

Joe is the keeper. The three men are :—

1. Slattery.
2. A Mr. Blennerhassett.
3. A Mr. Purfling.

Slattery I know already. He lives here, and is a permanent rod. I call him Slattery because it is not his name, and because I have always wished to know a man called Slattery, and I have never been so lucky. This is the best I can do. Slattery is a man of science. He owns a motor-car and a billiard-table and a beautiful garden and a kind heart and Mrs. Slattery. Slattery is Fortune's pet. His business, however—there are drawbacks even to being Slattery—keeps him from the river all day; but by seven o'clock he is there. I shall see him at seven o'clock this evening, and it will be a good meeting.

Purfling I have yet to meet.

Mr. Blennerhassett dawned upon me this morning, at the Lower End.

Before I permit him to dawn upon you, let me say something of the Lower End. I want you to know this length of the Clere because it is the most beautiful place in the world. Thus, as we go along I propose to do my best—my insufficient, my miserably insufficient best—to make you see it all as I see it.

I fancy that the sadness which sharpens our delight in any rarely beautiful experience arises from our knowledge that it is not to be captured. We are doomed to lose it. There is to be no putting of it away in a drawer, whence we shall be able to take it out and relive it again and again. Presently it will be gone, and no trick or force of memory shall bring it back. Again, we feel the hopelessness of any such attempt. These exquisite things of the senses may not be translated into any such cumbrous medium as language. But though we despair, we try.

Of the Lower End, then, I will say that it is broad and deep, dark, heavily weeded, flowing leisurely between rushes and reed beds and withy beds, under thick woods of beech and aspen and willow; a water for great fishes (not many), unfriendly to small, not to be netted, pike haunted.

It is a region that well fits the frame of mind
induced by black, thundery weather, when the
water looks like lead, and the trout lie on the
bottom, and there is no fly, and one has smoked
one's last cigarette. Yet in sunshine and in this
early season it has a beauty that the more open
water above lacks, a beauty of shadow and colour,
when the light filters yellow-green through young
beech leaves, and mingles with the brown-green
that the river weeds reflect upwards where the
jewelled heart of the wood joins the glowing
depth of the stream.

From one bank lush water-meadows spread
away to the foot of the downs, and the stuggy,
good-natured pollards stand in rows along the
ditches and lead the eye unenviously to tremendous
elms, shadowing the valley road. Yes, if you
turn your back on the river (he will take no offence)
the scenery is cheerful enough. Here the Valley
is broader than above, the wind has a freer sweep
and the clouds seem to sail more steadily; and the
cuckoos, I swear, fly here and shout more vigor-
ously. I have often been wonderfully uplifted at
the Lower End. There is no part of the water
where meditation (an important branch of dry-fly
angling) may be practised with less chance of
interruption, and there is no part which I do
more heartily love. For here the days begin.

Such was the scene of · my encounter with
Mr. Blennerhassett.

I had been waiting during two hours for something to happen. At last it happened. It was a
very unpromising little ring, but (because one
never knows) I cast over it two or three times.
Then I sat down waiting for it to happen again.

Something else happened.

Down the bank—the bank, mark you! not the
meadow—two feet from the verge, as I live—
came striding a handsome, healthy young man,
ruddy, caparisoned for angling. He held his
head high, his chest thrown out. A moustache
bristled upwards from his lips. As he perceived
me a look of haughty disdain disfigured his
personable face. He came forward authoritatively.
A willow forced him out of the direct path, and
so, without disturbing my fish (if it was still there),
he reached my side. He was good enough to
inquire if I had done anything. I said that I had
just failed to hook a fish. He said that he hadn't
seen a damned thing all morning. I asked if this
was Mr. Blennerhassett. He said it was, and
asked me what was the best fly. I told him
what I thought was the best fly. He asked
me what I thought was the best place at this
time of day. I told him the Mill, which is at
the extreme top of the water. He said he had

already been there, and there wasn't a damned fish moving. I expressed my regret.

At this moment a little ring appeared in the water just where I was looking for it.

" A rise ! " said Mr. Blennerhassett. " A rise, by God ! "

He knelt down and began to switch out line. I passed my hand over my eyes. I thought that I was mad. I was not. When I removed my hand he was covering my fish. It was a deft cast. The fish rose ; subsided.

" A damned dace," said Mr. Blennerhassett, reeling in.

I was quite dumb.

" Well," he observed, " I'll get on up the water." I wished him good sport. He strode away without replying. I observed him halt almost immediately, and begin to make very long casts towards the further bank, where I had been expecting a fish to show itself for half an hour.

My fish again rose. It was, as Mr. Blennerhassett had surmised, a dace. As I returned the poor little thing I heard my new acquaintance furiously shouting. " Have you a net ? " he bellowed. I saw that his rod was bent.

I was now compelled to run up the bank with a net for this Blennerhassett. When I arrived I found that his trout was in the weeds. The water was about five feet deep.   It was not, however, necessary for him to order me into it, because the fish disentangled itself and came to the bank and was peremptorily knocked on the head.   I congratulated the Blennerhassett.

He left me instantly.

I wonder what Purfling is like.

V

OF TWO KEEPERS

I HAVE said that Joe is our keeper.

He keeps the fishes, and the birds and hares and rabbits on the downs, but he makes no parade of these accomplishments. He also keeps the hedges in order and the peace among his fellow-servants on the estate. There is nothing to which he will not and cannot turn his hand. I have known him to spend three days in painting a roof of corrugated iron sky-blue. Now the men who have done that can be numbered on your fingers. He can cart coals better than anyone alive. With his slow smile he can make a day of east wind promising. He is a lovely man. With this prodigality of talent he is competent in every-thing that he undertakes. He has no false ideas about the comparative dignity of employment. Anything that is work is good enough for him, though it be the emptying of a cesspool. Such distasteful labour he undertakes without a thought of his place, thereby glorifying it and making it worthy of him. I have never heard him say an

unkind word of any living soul—or dead one, for
that matter. He tolerates everybody, rejoices
in their successes, unaffectedly laments their dis-
appointments. Of an evening he takes his
relaxation among the rabbits. And he cannot
fish, and never attempts to accompany an angler.

I say, he cannot fish.

And he never attempts to accompany an angler.

I will now tell you of another river keeper, that
you may understand the fullness of the last-named
virtues which are Joe's.

This adventure befell me because one night
a kindly-disposed man offered me a day on some
priceless water which he had in Hampshire. I
was going to Scotland or Manchester or one of
those places where there are no chalk streams
almost immediately, but I could just sandwich in
my day if I took it on the morrow. Therefore
I hardly went to bed at all, and at the hour when
I was in the habit of recomposing myself to the
slumber from which a persistent yet dispirited
housemaid had waked me, I got out of the down
train into God's second county.

The wind blew soft from the south-west, and
the sky looked as if the sun were scotched for the
day. I told myself that I should certainly catch
a great many trout, and I almost believed it.
I swore that an angler's is the only incomparable

life, and as I took the high road through the valley I kicked up the dust in clouds for sheer high spirits. This was to be a day of days. And so I came to the cottage of William Pound.

I was naturally anxious to reach the water at the earliest possible moment, but Courtesy required me to report myself to William, and Nature demanded a breakfast at the Inn. Afterwards I desired to go away by myself and fish. But when I had found William, and had satisfied him of my right to take the lives of his employer's trout (if I could), and had mentioned that I would go and get some food, and that I supposed I should see him later on—which means, in plain English, that I would be happy to compensate him for the loss of my society during the day by a suitable gift at the end of it—when, I say, I had done all this, and made as if to leave him, he asserted that there was no use in fishing before 10.30, and invited me to visit his crops of vegetables. Now I had deprived myself so far of a hot breakfast and of several hours' sleep in order to gain the riverside by 9.30, and I had no wish to contemplate William's orderly rows of beetroots, lettuces, and cabbages, or even potatoes. My soul was attuned to less earthly things. I felt, however, that a refusal must be churlish, and I consented. Here I made a vital mistake, for from that moment William had me at his mercy.

It was nearly half-past nine, when, having brought his last cauliflower to my notice, William gave me permission to seek my breakfast. He would call for me at the Inn at ten. This was the moment for speaking up. I should have said: "William, do not call for me at ten; do not follow me to the river. I shall do capitally alone. Do not put yourself out on my account. Stay here, William, and cultivate your garden." But I had not the courage to say this. It were easier to decline an invitation to Windsor. There is no doubt that he felt that in accompanying me he would be doing me not so much a service as an honour, and to hint that I would rather be without him was beyond me. "But he will quickly tire," I reflected, "of seeing me blundering about and putting down rising fish. He will stay an hour at the most. I shall soon be alone." And I agreed to wait for him at the Inn till ten. As I ate my eggs and toast I indulged in the hope that after all William might find wire-worms among his carnations, and as I put up my rod and greased my line in the porch, that hope grew stronger with each minute which brought the hand of the clock nearer to the hour, for still no glimpse of William was visible upon the road.

D

At ten precisely he was with me, nor did he forget
ponderously to draw out his watch by way of
emphasising his punctuality.

We were presently beside a small backwater.
" Here," said William, " we can begin to fish.
This rod," he continued (taking it from my hand),
" is no good.   I have one up at my cottage which
is worth ten of he."   So saying, he selected a fly
from his cap, tied it on, and oiled it—all with
great deliberation.   " You won't find it easy
under this tree, sir," he remarked, as he got out
line.   " There be a whopper lays under that elder.
Shall I try for 'un ? "   It was at this point that
I ought to have said : " No, William; I will."
But he did not wait for my answer, and I could
not snatch the rod out of his very hands.   He
rose the fish and appeared well satisfied.   " Told
'ee so, sir," he said.   " Now do 'ee cast in among
they flags."   I was glad enough to recover the
rod, and fished for some minutes without success.
" My, what a whop ! " said William, though I
could see for myself that the fly had not touched
the water very lightly.   Presently he said : " We'd
best get down to the bottom of thick meadow.
Main stream be easier fer 'ee."   Down there we
found some fly, and a rising trout, over which
I made a number of infamous casts, to the
accompaniment of William's " Too fur to the

right. Not up to un. 'Ee won't find 'un there,
sir. My! what a whop!" and other encouragements. Finally, " Let me have a whack," said he,
and in sheer curiosity to see if he could cheat the
wind and the drag and the trout all together,
I gave place to him. Neither the wind nor the
drag seemed to present any difficulties to William,
though the trout would not come up, and for
twenty minutes I was witness of an exhibition of
skill which I gladly confess was of the finest
quality. What he would have done with the rod
up at the cottage I do not know, but with mine
he did about fifty things which I shall never learn
to do if I fish till I am a hundred—which is
William's age.

The sight of a rise in a very attractive spot gave
me courage to ask for a turn, and so I got a
nice fish. " Now," said I, in a foolish burst of
generosity, "you must get one." Nothing rose
for the next two hundred yards, but William
fished the water carefully up to a bridge on which
I sat smoking and marvelling at his dexterity. It
was mid-day, and the fly was fairly off the water
when he left me to go and get a bit of dinner.
He promised to be back in an hour. Had I
possessed a spark of courage, I should have told
him plainly not to come back. I should have
reminded him that I had come all the way from

London to fish, and not to sit about and watch
him doing it. But my chance of taking a firm
stand had gone by, and I could only swear to
make the most of my lonely hour. Of it three-
quarters passed without incident, and then I
got to work on a fair fish that rose irregularly,
at what I do not know. I put, perhaps, five flies
over him, and was just tying on an alder when I
observed the massive figure of William moving remorselessly towards me across the water-meadows.
In three minutes he was angling for that trout.
Now I had found it and fished for it, and by all
the rules of the game it was mine to catch or
put down. But I was too cowed to protest. I
am not man enough for Williams and Blenner-
hassetts and people like them. William tried fly
after fly, fishing with such delicacy and precision
that I almost forgave him. At last he tied on
what he called a drake's hare's ear. I did not
know the fly, but it looked a likely one, and I
up and asserted myself, clutched the rod which he
had laid very incautiously on the grass, and at the
second throw had the exquisite pleasure of landing
the fish before William's eyes.

I was now at peace with all the world, and
yielded up the rod without a murmur. At four
o'clock William had landed two fish and risen
three others, and was engaged at an angle of

the stream up to his knees in water (where I could not follow him) over three good trout which he said he could see. Every now and then he would answer me when I spoke, and sometimes when I coughed he would tell me how he was getting on. But most of the time he was quite unconscious of my presence on the bank, and I am sure that he was very happy. I was wet and cold and hungry by this time, and I left him (he hardly turned his head) and went away to the Inn for tea. On my return he was still at the same place. The food must have given me heart, for I found myself able to claim the rod, and in a very short time William had discovered a trout and I had caught it. The custom was now thoroughly established, that after I had grassed a fish William was to have the rod, and I followed him up the stream till 6.30, when he took me to a stretch of water which we had not yet visited. Here there was no fly, so from that time I had the rod to myself until it was too dark for me to see, when William resumed it, and finished the day with an exhibition of long casting under the far bank, in the course of which the spear of the butt fell into the long grass and was lost to me for ever.

Joe would have been far too busy mowing to treat me in such a way. Besides, morally and practically he is incapable of it.

VI

OF PAINTING IN WATER-COLOURS

IT is now a little less than a year since I followed the making of a water-colour sketch from its first rough pencil lines to its signature. The young man who made it, my friendship for whom, up to that moment, had never been clouded by any reverence whatever, assumed wholly new proportions in my sight. The air with which he produced his materials, his Whatman board, his brushes, his water-pot, his sponge and his worn palette, glorified by the deposits from masterly mixtures, his confidence as he began taking measurements of the Ocean (by which we sat) along his marvellously sharpened pencil, the ease with which he roughed in his outlines, the vigour of his attack upon the sky, his deft handling of rocks and breakers, these things gave me food for thought, "Is it, then," I reflected, "that this adolescent has been enjoying up to now a consideration at my hands totally inadequate to his real parts? Is it possible that one whom I have

38

known from the cradle should be master of such
mysteries?" And lo! he had ended, and the
vasty deep was mine to hang in the drawing-
room. I was compelled to own that the impossible had happened. The boy had painted a
picture, a picture, by Neptune! which breathed
salt air like an onshore gale.

After my first stunned feeling had passed away,
other reflections came to me. "Since," I thought,
"a friend of mine can learn in his spare time to
produce results so remarkable, it is clear that the
trick is easier of acquirement than' I supposed.
After all, many young girls with no more brains
than their sisters do produce most tolerable
sketches, and it is not to be supposed that they
devote more than a small proportion of their
leisure to gaining their facility. Golf and lawn
tennis, croquet and district visiting, these and
other amusements claim them visibly for many
of their waking hours, yet they produce pictures
of which no one can mistake the meaning. Here,
one shall say with certainty, is the representation
of a lake with undoubted swans; this can only
figure a distant mountain, and if these streaks and
gloom be not like a sunset behind a churchyard,
they are like nothing. Go to!" I said. "Let us
emulate these damsels."

I conceived a contempt for water-colour sketching. I thought that I, even I, might be capable of it.

A year has passed, or almost a year. At length I find myself where perfect isolation may be secured for several hours at a time. This is a condition precedent to my assault upon the realm of pictorial art, for an observer of my deeds would utterly blight my endeavours. I must take my first steps quite alone.

A man—one of the few disagreeable men I know—once told me that when he sees anyone painting in the open air his genius prompts him to go behind the artist, regard the picture for a while, and then, with a heavy sigh, turn away. Suppose someone should come and do this behind me.

I must find a very secret spot.

The river will furnish me with what I want.

Disguised as an angler, rod in hand, creel on hip, waders well displayed, I will walk boldly into the meadows. No one hereabouts will give me a second thought. But if they should know what my creel contains, I feel that they would come trooping to gape and snigger at my back.

Until I can manage my materials (purchased by stealth last week—I too have my Whatman board, my brushes, my paint-box, my sponge, my palette) I will paint nothing but willows and rushes and water and the reflections in water, and the gleams of weed beneath it. A certain dexterity having been acquired among these simple subjects, I will with less trepidation attempt to limn the thatch and brick of the populous village.

.   .   .   .   .   .

I have now sketched in water-colours.

.   .   .   .   .   .

I have been looking through the catalogue of artists' materials, very generously included free of charge with my recent purchases, and particularly at the list of colours. My unsuccess is now explained. The tubes that have been sold to me are dull, commonplace things. Cobalt Blue, Yellow Ochre, Vandyke Brown, Dragon's Blood, Raw Sienna, Burnt Sienna. These names carry me back nearly half a century to the nursery where, with a shilling box of paints, I tinted the designs of the then fashionable Kate Greenaway. How should I have rendered sedgy banks and feathery willows and elusive tremulous reflections with such trite matter? What I need is a supply of Oxide of Chromium and Italian Pink, Mars Yellow and Scarlet Madder Alizarin, Hooker's Green No. 2, and Purple Lake and Primrose Aureolin. The very names are an inspiration. What effects I might achieve with these! How truly I could paint with Constant White! How imperishably with Permanent Mauve! How strenuously with Intense Blue! My sketch gives me no pleasure when I regard it. Let me rather gloat in anticipation over these marvels of the colourman. Let me fill up order forms.

VII

OF CHAVENDER, TEA-DRINKING, AND THE BEST ANGLER

CHAVENDER has been here fishing, and has caught more fishes than I believed it possible for one man to draw out of this river in the space of three days. Every afternoon he has been driven into the house, about tea-time, by the intolerable burden of trout with which his creel has been stuffed; then, having discharged his cargo, he has swallowed about ten cups of tea and departed, to be seen no more until dinner, when, the larder having been further enriched and a hasty meal having been swallowed, he has once more put forth to the work, and night has fallen upon him still slaughtering. This is the kind of guest that it is a real pleasure to have in the house. Until his return for the night to these premises our conversational labours with Chavender are limited to an affable good morning, and his, with us, to a request for the salt or more tea. But his waders once off, he will talk like a Christian and show no signs of restlessness till any hour of the morning that it may happen to be when we make him go to bed. Thus by day my wife and I are able to pursue our ordinary avocations just as if Chavender were not here, and by night we are compelled, by the laws of hospitality, to indulge our passion for frivolous talk to most improper lengths.

Chavender is distinguishable from other men by (1) his power of catching fishes, (2) his capacity for tea-drinking. Teapots turn pale at Chavender. He empties them. That is what he does with them. He is their master. We have a little small teapot which is really a coffee-pot. This was sent up to Chavender's bedroom on his first morning here. He must have used it with frightful rigour, for nothing has been able to persuade it to venture again into his chamber. Now only the largest and strongest of these vessels ever goes there. When a teapot is confronted with Chavender it shrivels up and becomes nothing at all. Let it be accustomed to hold tea for ten, twice. Chavender fixes it with his eye, and the poor thing is bolting out of the room crying for a fresh supply. Only one man has driven a pen big enough for Chavender and the teapots, and he definitely gave up writing centuries ago. I have therefore borrowed his giant quill—the good fellow made no bones about letting me have it—for that which follows. But one writer, one pen. I am not man enough for his, not though I take both arms to it. As witness:

Then he called for tea. And thenceforward for the space of one thousand and five hundred and sixty and three or four minutes, to be strictly accurate, there was such a pumping of pumps, kindling of fires, boiling of kettles, such a milking of cattle—Jerseys, shorthorns, Bedfordshires, black, brown, white, yellow, spotted with dun and splashed with red, fat, lean, with crumpled horn and with horn of symmetrical shape, and Chilling-hams, not to mention buffaloes and yaks and female coiros (of which there are too few); such an opening of caddies and measuring of measures, such a filling of sugar-bowls, such an outgoing of the raw material, such a polishing and rubbing up of spoons and knives, such a submitting to the towel of cups and platters, such a disintegration of loaves, wheaten and oaten, such a spreading of butter, such a bringing of cakes—seed, currant, sultana, and the Simnel and the Genoa cakes and all other kinds of cakes and Dundee cake, such a spreading of tray cloths, such an unfolding of Japanese napkins, such a making and a baking of little brown scones and cookies and other hot breads, that the like was never seen before nor

shall ever be seen again. Then he began to drink.
Eternal swilling of fragrant liquor! Oh! the
great cups he took off one after the other! How
they evaporated in front of him! They came,
and they were not. It was like the ocean assimi-
lating rivers. What inversions of china! What
journeys they made! More tea, good lady. Fill
it out. Spare not of pouring, sweet hostess, for
God made the tea-tree for this very purpose. As
I suck tea, it is a great drink! I have killed fishes
all day, but now I will absorb. To the kitchen
with you, stout host. Though there be no bells
in this house, yet will I tickle it off. Watch me
to do it. 'Tis a thing worth learning. There!
it is gone, the precious reviving stuff. And more
is to come. What is the rain for but to appease
my desire? It has percolated through much
earth, but now it is in my interior. Host, to
the back premises with you. There is a fresh
brewing required. Cups! Cups! Bring me tea
in a bath!

It is not only in the afternoon that Chavender
exhibits these prodigies. Ten at night is his prin-
cipal time for tea-drinking. And he sleeps like
a child after it. A single cup will keep me waking
till dawn; therefore I envy Chavender, and write
in this way about him. I am allowed no tea at
night. I am offered bananas by the dispenser

of tea. Bananas! while Chavender gurgles with
tea. Oh! I detest favouritism.

I wonder what the fellow's nerves are like.
While he sits there drinking I could cheerfully
see him opened up by the medical men who would
tell me. "If this much stimulant," I ask myself,
"only serves to bedew the eyelids of Chavender
with the balmiest of sleep, what would happen
were he deprived of it? It is clear that he would
never wake up at all. And then his companionship would be lost to us. So I comfort myself
for the partiality of the tea-dispenser.

I have said that Chavender always catches fish
in this river. He employs honourable methods.
He is, therefore, a good fisherman. This conclusion is open to objection, as thus. It is not certain
that a man may not be a good fisherman and yet
catch few fish. A good fisherman is one who
fishes well. Results have nothing to do with it.

I reply that results have everything to do with
it. A man who fishes well without catching fish
is a contradiction in terms. Mechanical skill in
the casting of flies may be acquired on a water
that is quite empty of fishes. Similarly, a man
may learn by heart all the practical hints of all
the anglers who have ever written until there is
nothing he cannot tell you about barbel-bait and
the respective merits of gorge and snap-tackle for

pike and the habits of eels. But the winner of
casting tournaments is not, from that fact alone,
a good angler. He is a long caster. And the
student is very seldom a good angler. He gains
distinction in a totally different field. He is in
the same plane of existence with the Astronomer,
the Classic, and Mr. Datas. I do not say that the
Fly-casting Champion or the diligent reader of
angling books cannot be also a good angler, but
if he is, it is not by reason of his medals or his
library.

An angler—let us confine ourselves to chalk-
stream fishing—a chalk-stream angler may be a
good caster of flies, may have a good knowledge
of water insects and of the fishes' ways, and yet
not be a good chalk-stream angler. He may be a
good strategist as well, and a good man to boot,
but unless he catches fish (honourably always
understood) he is not a good angler. Again, I do
not insist on his always catching fish. There are
days when the Sainted Peter himself should
return with an empty creel. But any man who
can go forth day after day to this teeming stream
and not have trout or graylings to show, though
he cast like Marryat and know like Francis, I say
that he is a bad fisherman. Something is wrong.
Such a man will come in at night with nothing
but a tale of woe. There was no fly; there was

too much sun; the water was two degrees too cold; the wind was wrong; the weeds were the very devil. Such fish as he rose he covered perfectly at the first cast, but they all came short, or the light was awkward and he didn't see his fly as it fell. Perhaps he got his hook in, but it was in too lightly; or the fish, a very strong one, went to weed in spite of all he could do to prevent it. He winds up with an explanation of the lack of fly or a dissertation upon weed-cutting. But he takes no fishes. Such—saving only the Marryat-like casting and the Francis-like knowledge—am I.

Chavender, arriving a moment later, pours out a brace of trout weighing four and half pounds. He can afford to keep silent as to his failures, of which there have been many no doubt, so he offers no excuses. He never offers excuses, holding rightly that if there is any blame to be bestowed it belongs to the angler more than anywhere else. Excuses only make incompetence more evident. To say that a fish went to weed is, in other words, to say that the angler was unable to stop him. And as it would be ridiculous to criticise the fish for seeking to escape, if criticism is necessary at all, it must be directed upon the fisherman. A complete reticence about these disasters is the seemly conduct.

E

I have accompanied Chavender while he has been fishing, and from observations made I have come to the conclusion that the best angler is not the man who combines the finest casting with the greatest knowledge, the rarest patience with the deadliest guile, the most unyielding resolution with the brightest enthusiasm, but simply he who makes the fewest mistakes.

Chavender catches fish to which I have cast easily (at the fifth trial when they were no longer there), for whose capture my knowledge should have been adequate, which have not unduly tried my patience, nor made great demands on my craftiness, nor my resolution. As for enthusiasm, mine has burned high just before I have failed to catch these fishes. A chalk-stream trout is often to be found the day after one has put him down, in the same place, rising to the same kind of fly, under the same kind of conditions. Such trout I have indicated to Chavender, and he has grassed them. Why? Because he has made no mistake. He has waited for a cloud, he has waited for a lull, he has taken note of the weed-beds, he has taken note of the probabilities of drag, he has made a rough guess at the number of duns which that fish lets go by; in short, he has made his dispositions, reducing the chances of failure to the minimum. Then, deliberately, he has cast and, everything being in his favour and the fly lighting correctly, the fish has risen, and has been hooked. Chavender has a mental chart of the river bed and his surroundings on the bank, and this enables him with the least possible amount of trouble to bring the fish to the landing stage. (I speak as if it were a steamboat, but no matter.) The net is put into the water at the right moment, never too soon; the fish is grassed, considered, bludgeoned, or returned. All this quite without flurry. If the creature escapes, Chavender does not explain. He turns a little white and goes on to another, master, as far as is possible in angling, of himself and of his destiny.

It could never happen to Chavender to fall thrice into the same ditch while endeavouring to get a tight line on a trout. Chavender would know the ditch was there, and would run down stream between it and the river rather than backwards into the ditch, as I did yesterday week. Yes, Chavender makes fewer mistakes than any other angler I know, and that is why he is the best.

You may argue, if you please, that if this contention is pushed as far as it will go, the best angler is the man who never fishes, and so makes fewer mistakes even than Chavender. But I say tush to you. Can anyone be more mistaken than the man who never fishes? And I say bah to you.

.   .   .   .   .   .

Another virtue in Chavender. He encourages the painter that I feel is in me. He has said: "You have clearly reached a stage where you are fit to take lessons." This seems complimentary. There are then painters, worse than I, who are absolutely unfit to receive instruction. I am comforted. I do not grudge Chavender his tea to-night.

.   .   .   .   .   .

I have sent six pictures to a professional painter who, Chavender assures me, will return, within a few posts, criticisms which I shall value, instruction which will enable me to exhibit next summer at Burlington House, and praise, which I must have.

VIII

OF PURFLING AND PURISM

I HAVE met Purfling.

A little while ago, coming across Slattery's lawn where it borders the river, I saw a man standing on the wooden bridge at the top of the shallow. I always approach this bridge with hosannahs on my lips; it is in such a very beautiful place. Here the Valley opens out suddenly. Great meadows, among which the river saunters, and great elms and the two downs that close the view—the one round and green, the other capped with its clump and streaked red with plough land — compose the prospect upstream. Beyond the downs, right in the broad V they make, the sun sets on summer evenings, and out of the sunset the red quills float towards one, and in the lit water broad black rings appear. Crab Hatch is just round the corner, and Crab Hatch holds the fathers of the stream.

This is the best bit of the river.

The man on the bridge stood very still. His back was towards me. His accoutrements proclaimed him an angler. I arrived and jovially greeted him.

He returned my salutation; coldly, I thought. I said, "Are you Mr. Purfling?" He admitted that he was. In my own name he appeared to take no interest, so I told it to him. He said, "Ah!"

Now when "Ah!" is all a man has to say about your name, you detest him. I detested Purfling, but I went on being polite. I asked if there was any fly showing yet. He replied that he had seen one female *Baetis rhodani*. A suspicion entered my mind. I thanked him for the information, and said that it sounded a rather difficult insect to imitate. "For myself," I added, "I generally stick on an Olive Dun here at this time of the morning in May." He smiled indulgently. "I see," he said, "that I ought to have said Olive Dun." "It would have been better," said I. "I am no scholar." I began to grease my line with a piece of ham fat which I had cut off for that purpose at breakfast, having forgotten to bring any vaseline to Willows. When I had smeared it all over the line and my hands and my trousers, I looked up to find him regarding me with obvious contempt.

"Don't you find that rather tiresome every day?" he asked. "If you would dress your line properly in the winter you would never have to mess about with fat and things. A pint of shellac dissolved in ten ounces of beeswax and boiled for three hours with an equal quantity of bear's grease, ketchup, spermaceti, liquorice, and rain-water, strained through butter muslin, and——"

"I am no cook," said I, "but it is kind of you to give me the recipe." So it was. People always mean kindly when they teach other people their business. My suspicion grew. To make quite sure, I asked, "Have you done anything yet?" He stiffened. "There has been no fly," he replied, in the voice with which people are put in theit places. Then he went away.

It is even so.

Purfling is a Purist.

I am not a Purist.

The art by which I humbly seek to earn my bread induces, or should induce, the habit of observation. Thus I am an observer of men, and among men of fishermen, and among fishermen of dry-fly fishermen.

Purfling being gone, let us lean together on this wooden bridge — the rail is exactly the most comfortable height — and let me discourse to

you awhile of purism and purists and things
puristic.

Youth, sir, is proverbially avid of pleasure, and
seeks it in a hundred ways, which experience
abandons one by one. There was a time when
I believed in all honesty that I could gain enjoyment by climbing hills, and in that belief I have
struggled to the tops of several mountains. Presently reason triumphed, another illusion was dis-
carded, and I had advanced one further stage in
that eliminating process by which human happiness alone can be reached. Now, while in one
short summer I mastered the true secret of the
hills—that they were made to be admired from
below—I also learned another fact about them:
that there is always one more summit to be
climbed. So with angling.

When, as a child, I threaded my hooks through
the unprotesting lips of living minnows in the
hope of luring the great chubs of the Kennet, I
knew that men far more skilful than I used spinning baits for jack; and I told myself that one day
I should be a man and do likewise. Later, promoted
to spinning, I lusted ardently to angle with flies
for trout. Then, a loch-fisher, I dreamed of chalk-
streams and the mysteries of the floating fly.
"There," I said, "is the summit, the *ne plus ultra*,
the last rung," and I vowed ere I died to make one

of the elect. So when my destiny did indeed
bring me to the side of the Darenth with a split
cane rod and a floating line (well greased, believe
me) and a little bottle of oil at my button and
a boxful of assorted duns and a season's permit in
my pocket, you may be sure that I was inclined
very scornfully to regard the unintelligent horde
who, with their clumsy casts of three, lash the
waters of the north country. I thought that I
had arrived. I had not. From the dizzy heights
to which I had mounted I looked backwards and
downwards to where the groundlings, whose company I had quitted for ever, plied their dull tasks,
and had never a thought, in my ignorance and
arrogance, for the cold, clear, distant peaks which
lay above my head, whose very existence I did
not suspect, to which I now know I shall never
climb.

For though I have fished chalk-streams for
many years, I am still a bungler, and a bungler I
shall live and die. They say that there is always
room at the top. This is not the case. To attain
the highest in any abstract science, such as dry-fly
fishing can become, a man must be made of rarer
clay than mine. There is in my nature an ineradi-
cable thirst for the death of fishes which shall
for ever exclude me from the company of

that esoteric few who practise the utmost refinements.

To come at last to my subject. I seem to discover seven separate degrees of dry-fly [angling. The lowest fisherman of this kind is the man who is absolutely learning his art. He is content with little results. A single fish is ample reward for a day's toil. A couple of brace sets him quite above himself, and he boasts all winter of a two-pounder. He carries a steelyard in his pocket, and to its test (that every ounce may tell) he submits every fish instantly on its being taken. He spends more than he can afford on the charming little japanned boxes which the tackle-makers sell. He has many hundreds of flies, and presents each pattern patiently to each rising trout until the list, or the fish, becomes exhausted. This tactless fool asks his masters to let him see the fishes they have caught. He cannot understand their reasons for returning them. A fish to him is a fish, and he is not nice in the matter of its colour, rotundity, or sex. The ideal of three brace of eighteen-inch males would never present itself to his mind. He is not æsthetic at all.

A little higher in the scale is the ordinary angler, such as I am; the man who can take a trout now and then when things are going right; who feels a certain reluctance to kill fishes that are not in the pink of condition, yet at times of scarcity is known to allow his baser nature to get the better of that reluctance ; who in the morning nurses an ambition to bring home a heavy basket ; who carries no steelyard, but prefers to allow, in stating the weight of his fish, for the ounces which they lose after death ; who employs habitually but few patterns, yet will not disdain in obstinate cases to bring out fancy lures. This man is met with everywhere.

Above him is found the three-fly expert. Two shades of olive and a black gnat are enough for him. He will allow himself a Mayfly when it is on the water, but at other seasons he is rigid. He casts each pattern but once, for, so supreme is his skill, what are called " trial casts " are unknown to his fishing. He calls trout " fario," and possesses a secret recipe for the dressing of a line. Such an one I suspect yonder Purfling to be.

I now come to the point where the taint of blood at last ceases to pollute the fair name of dry-fly fishing. The anglers of whom I have spoken still move upon a lower plane. They all try to catch and kill trout. But with my next example the regions of pure science are entered. For it is, or so I believe, this very point of slaughter which marks off the truly great angler from the merely expert. Yet here again are degrees of greater and less perfection. Fourthly, then, I find the man who fishes for the single purpose of successfully deceiving the trout into the belief that he is going to eat a living fly—in other words, he fishes for rises. When he addresses himself to his work he is moved by no wish to see his prey— he seeks no prey—gasping upon the grass. He sits down before none but the oldest and most circumspect of fishes, those fishes which are the despair of other, of lesser anglers. He will pass a summer casting over one of these, and he will count his time well spent can he but persuade it to open its mouth to him once. He is calm in the presence of the loaded creels of his fellows, for he knows that for him are joys of a rarer and more essential quality than any that visit their degraded bosoms.

I am now getting on to very high ground. My fifth angler takes his pleasure through a pair of field-glasses. It is his to watch the trout and their ways. He sits by the stream, purged of every thought save the acquirement of know-ledge. It is to him that we owe the priceless information that a trout will rise at other objects than living insects; small twigs, for example, scraps of straw—yes, and the petals of flowers.

Is it possible, you ask, that angling can be carried yet higher? The number seven was mentioned, and here we are fishing through binoculars in five steps. Have patience. These things unfold themselves slowly.

One more stage, and the supereminent is just beyond. Sport is, after all, only the handmaid of natural history. It is good to seek healthy recreation, but it is better to serve humanity. The pursuit of birds, beasts, and fishes is in itself an end to lower natures. Yet there is a savagery about it which must revolt the Thinker. To know—that is the highest object of man's energy; and to know the trout aright we must know on what he feeds. The angler, then, to whom I would now direct your attention, having mastered the things that the fish of his chosen study does, turns his mind to the things that it eats. He moves on by one other degree towards perfection. He catches flies.

Lastly—and here I reach the supreme point to which (so far as I know) the science of dry-fly fishing has attained—lastly is found the all-knowing fisherman who, abandoning rod, creel, waders, trout, flies, and river as matters which no longer concern the investigator, occupies his angling hours in the loving study of the habits of the birds. Beyond this I do not think fishing can go. Yet mathematicians tell us that there is a fourth dimension of existence inconceivable to common minds, only dimly suspected by the rarest, and it may be that there are other and still higher regions to which it is possible for the angler to attain. Who knows ?

IX

OF CERTAIN TUBES AND A FAIR PROSPECT

THE colours which I ordered the other day
have come. Now in my box I have—

Constant White.

Italian Pink.

Permanent Mauve.

Purple Lake.

Hooker's Green, No. 1.

Hooker's Green, No. 2.

Intense Blue.

Scarlet Madder Alizarin.

Mars Yellow.

Oxide of Chromium.

Primrose Aureolin.

This is better. I shall set to work with something like confidence now. This morning I will
paint the valley from the top of the Beacon
Down. But first I must make me a new palette.

.   .   .   .   .   .

Here we are, sir. This is the ·Beacon Down,
and, I think you'll admit, a notable place for a

signal fire. Surely the whole of Wiltshire can
see us up here. Ay, and Hants and Dorset to
boot—and you can see them if you will, the one
south, the other west; and if you have any
imagination to pierce that soft blue circle of haze
of which we are the centre, you shall see Somerset
and Gloucester and Oxford and all the other
noble counties of England. Yes, here we are,
with nothing between us and God's sky, and no
sound in our ears but the calling of the larks and
the song of this clean wind in the grasses.

And my exasperating chatter? Certainly.

So! Sit there—a cigarette?—and fill your
eyes while I get my painting things out. For
I am not at all daunted by this landscape—now
that my new colours have come.

.   .   .   .   .   .

You perceive, sir, that this Beacon Down has
got in the way of our river. Hence this large
horseshoe bend that the Clere makes there below
us. Now you can see the whole of the water that
I fish. There's the mill, beside the church tower
among the elms, where that small road has just
crawled down through the chalk hills from Little
Harmony to meet the valley highway. And
there is Willows just below us. Do you mark
the thatch of our cottage, there, between the

copper beech that is the pride of Mrs. Slattery's heart and the Five Poplars. And you can see Slattery's lawn, the one by the river where the big forget-me-not beds are. And there, as I exist, is Mrs. Slattery with her scarlet parasol. And there's the island pool about a foot and a half below Mrs. Slattery. The fishes are rising greedily. Do I pretend to see them from this distance? Not at all. But am I not up here? What else, then, should they do but rise? Yet— what odds if they are rising? What odds if I *am* on Beacon Down and can't catch them. I can paint—that is, I can try to paint. Let them live! And I couldn't catch them if I were at the island pool. I know those fishes. I say, sir, let them live! Below, you will observe, at the Lower End the river turns again and is lost to sight. God speed it to the sea!

.   .   .   .   .   .

Yes, I *will* be talking.

I always talk when I am happy, and it makes me very happy to use my new colours. Let me tell you what I am painting, for I am already beginning to have my doubts about the picture as evidence of my employment of this morning.

From the mill upwards you see the Beaulieu water, the other half of the horseshoe; a mile

F

or more of it, right up to the next mill at Great
Ottley. There the beech wood behind the mill
thrusts out jealously from the downs to remind
us that the river is not the only thing worthy
of our admiration. Yet, were we angling to-day
and not painting, I would very gladly point out
to you the many excellent features of that water.
For I have never fished it, and my acquaintance
with it is purely imaginary. Yet with what
trouts and graylings have I furnished it as I have
sat up here and wandered in fancy where it shines
among its water - meadows — pulling them out.
That great red and grey Jacobean house is
Beaulieu (you know, I suppose, how to pronounce
that so as to be understood hereabouts), and that
is the park with its long green avenue of ancient
limes. And there is the Italian garden, all statues
and solemn trim hedges and fountains and
terraces, and to the right the old square, red-
walled fruit garden, and to the left the formal
pattern of the rose garden. It looks like a little
carpet from this high place.

You can see the tiny village of Beaulieu, there
by the end of the avenue. Six or seven houses
and a little inn, the "Three Moles" they call it.
But for these and their big house and the mill at
Great Ottley and the chimneys of Great Ottley
House (the next mansion in a valley of mansions),

there is not a habitation in sight. The valley is peopled with its trees—elms, Lombardy poplars, willows, aspens, limes, and ashes. And in between them the river and its full ditches glint perpetually. And if you will raise your eyes a little you may see the chalk country that lies behind these things, fold on fold of the green down-land, with the Seven Clumps at the Great Stones, the Seven Beech Clumps that mark the way for anyone who crosses the Plain from the south. And over all, in this fine north-westerly weather, the great clouds sail, throwing their shadows upon square miles of it.

That is what I am painting.

.   .   .   .   .   .

I have now used all my new colours except the Italian Pink. But there was nothing Italian in the landscape except the garden at Beaulieu, and that was not pink. Moreover, Italian Pink is not pink at all. It is a sort of yellowy brown. Perhaps there is some mistake. I must ask my instructor.

And still the result is not satisfactory.

.   .   .   .   .   .

Not even my wife's praise can make me wholly satisfied with my picture.

We had rain last night, and the valley was all new-washed this morning, and the sun, shining bravely, made everything very brilliant.

My picture, too, is very brilliant. But in a different way.

Have I been too lavish with the Mars Yellow?

X

OF A NEW VOICE IN THE VALLEY

THESE mornings I fish to slow music, for the
wind sits ever in the N.W. As I near the
island the breeze takes on a new kind of voice.
Its sigh becomes melodious; faint breaths of harmony intermingle with its whisper; its very lulls
are tuneful. Where, hitherto, the cuckoos and the
larks, the sheep and the cattle, the reeds and the
poplars alone have raised their untutored voices,
the meadows are vocal with arpeggios. The Spring
Song of Mendelssohn is distinguishable, sometimes
above, sometimes below that of the valley.

It is at this time of the day that my wife
practises.

Is there something in the harp which makes it
more akin to Nature than any other instrument?
In solitudes such as these one rarely hears any
human music. A piano may tinkle in a cottage
(for we are so excessively educated nowadays), a
travelling gramophone may stutter and wheeze
from the high road, a mouth-organ may go by at
the march, a hurdy-gurdy clatter out with im-

partial gusto a waltz or a hymn. These are the instruments of the countryside. Or a Flower Show may provide a brass band all the afternoon. And I have endured fiddling. This surely exhausts the list. Until I heard the harp thus, I denied the right of human beings to make music in chalk valleys. Let them keep to those rivers where men in starched collars punt girls under Japanese umbrellas. It does not matter to me that on such waters—more streets than streams— the banjo and the concertina, the mandolin, the cornet thump, wheeze, twang, and blare. I am not there. In this valley, however, I have always resented the intrusions of music—until now.

Whether the harp is really wilder than other instruments I cannot say. That it is this alleged savagery which renders it pleasing to my ear in this place I do not think. It may be so, but I have a suspicion that a 'cello or a flute, or a sackbut for that matter, under the same conditions, would be to me similarly agreeable. For when the harp sounds it sings to me of matters which lie entirely outside the scope of æsthetics. It is a new voice in the valley, and it carries messages to me which the old never reported. Perhaps to the wooing strains of Gounod's Serenade I seek to lure that four-pound trout which persists within the Island glide. Or, again, when I have risen and lost him, it is Consolation which celebrates the event.   But whatever the music and whatever the fortune, I am assured, by the harp, that everything that was once good is now a thousandfold better, and that there is nothing bad anywhere at all.

XI

OF NO CONSEQUENCE

THE professional painter has returned my picture with a first lesson, and the compliments for which I pant. Among other things, he has given me a strong caution against the use of the following colours:—

> Italian Pink,
> Mars Yellow,
> Scarlet Madder Alizarin,
> Both Hooker's Greens,
> Purple Lake,
> Primrose Aureolin,
> Constant White,
> Permanent Mauve,
> and
> Intense Blue.

Oxide of Chromium he admits to the palette. So my instinct was right. He has put me back on Vandyke Brown, Siennas, and other common old things. I expect I am not sufficiently adroit

for really interesting paints. But I hanker after
my Intense Blue. It cost me two shillings.

. . . . . .

It appears (I quote from my lesson) that trees
are not green. They are really Vandyke Brown
and Yellow Ochre and Burnt Sienna and Cobalt
Blue. I must verify this.

. . . . . .

There is a thing called the Essential Characteristic which resides in every object and distinguishes
it from everything else. Seize that, and nobody
can mistake what you have drawn, say a cathedral, for what you have not drawn, say an orange.
There is therefore something in a cathedral which
is not in an orange, and something in an orange
which is not in a cathedral. If these things be
discovered and properly drawn there is no chance
of your cathedral, however round and yellow,
being taken for an orange, nor your orange, let it
be as Gothic as it pleases, being admired as a
cathedral. The task which I must set myself is to
find these Essential Characteristics.

. . . . . .

After trial (upon white poplars and elms) I
make this assertion. Oranges and Cathedrals are
undistinguishable from each other.. It has been
well said that the study of art opens the eyes to

matters hitherto unsuspected. I can now believe
that trees are Vandyke Brown and Cobalt Blue
and all the other colours which my master men-
tions. If only there should be an Intense Blue
kind! I must ask him.

.   .   .   .   .   .

My Vandyke Brown has given out. Query?
Am I sufficiently adept to substitute for it my
Scarlet Madder Alizarin?

.   .   .   .   .   .

I had always believed the cow to be a very
nearly stationary beast. But a zoetrope is less
active.

.   .   .   .   .   .

Tree roots are better painted, covered with long
grass, especially the root of beeches. I wonder
with what long grass would be better covered when
one paints it.

.   .   .   .   .   .

It seems that if there is no red harp-string of
the required thickness, purple lake applied to a
yellow one does the trick.

XII

OF THE CLOUD ARTIST

THE Cloud Artist has been having a week's holiday and has left his job to the Rain Man, one of his two assistants. The other is the Blue Person. These functionaries are a discovery of my wife's. Between them they look after the arrangement of the sky. The Blue Person has had a long innings lately. Morning, noon, and evening he has spread his canvas, glowing azure overhead and at the edges soft purple, from one down to another. He had stolen a few little pink clouds from his Superior's store, and with these he would ornament his border from time to time, cleverly enough. He is a one effect man, yet the amazing beauty of what he does raises him above the charge of working in a groove. There are countries where he gets too much rope, and in such places they curse him for his monotony. England, favoured in so many ways, never sees the Blue Person too often, and his quite undeviating art meets with our hearty approval whenever he chooses to exercise it. As a matter of fact, the

Blue Person is not an artist at all. He is a canvas-stretcher just as the Rain Man is a maker of cloud in bulk for the Cloud Artist's use. So when the master is not in the studio, and the Rain Man is playing hookey, the Blue Person has it all his own way. If the Cloud Artist has an inspiration, then the Blue Person steps aside and we have pictures. Or perhaps the Rain Man comes rushing in and throws great lumps of his manufactures all over the Blue Person's pretty canvas, and then we put on mackintoshes.

A hill-top is the best stance for looking at the Cloud Artist's work. It is impossible to see too large an area of it. No one can paint in small compass better than he, and I have often framed a marvellous little six-foot-by-five with my bedroom window. But to see him as he should be seen one wants the whole vault of heaven. Then the fellow's infinite variety becomes properly apparent. I never can decide in which vein I prefer him. When he is doing his big bold work, with his great masses of cumulus, flinging them all day exuberantly across the blue, tearing continents of cloud to pieces and sending them swimming, he is at his liveliest and strongest. Then, too, he indulges his undoubted gift of humour. He becomes Rabelaisian, scolloping his edges into pompous, mile-long Bourbon faces, all chins, or pulling out bulging elephants and rocs and exaggerated humpy babies, and showing them to us and turning them into something different. My wife and I applaud him to the echo at such times, and would surely write letters to him thanking him for our entertainment, only we do not know his address. On cirrus days he is poetic, setting aloft filmy dreams in shell pink and pale gold, whose shapes the more ambitious kinds of birds have copied clumsily in their most delicate feathers, whose tints the more fragile sorts of flowers have tried to imitate in their petals. Earth, by gazing continually upwards and by striving her hardest to reproduce what she sees there, has succeeded in acquiring the beauty which we so much admire. The Alps, what are they but the expression of her desire to possess cumulus? And of a hot morning at Naples you may look over to Capri and see where she has almost achieved one of those soft blue mysteries which cost the Cloud Artist hardly a thought. And with what landscape can Earth rival his least-considered sunset display of purple plain and rosy hill and lake of molten gold?

I say nothing against the beauty of Earth. On the contrary, I spend a great deal of time here and elsewhere in extolling it. But I think that, being creatures of Earth, we push our admiration

of her too far.   There are men, who can ill afford
it, who buy weeks in Lovely Lucerne from Mr.
Cook—(the extent of human discomfort caused by
this person is shocking to contemplate)—and standing upon the Rigi Kulm, congratulate themselves
that modern civilisation has brought this marvel
within their reach for a five-pound note.   My wife
and I go up on to the Beacon Down, and, lying
very comfortably on our backs, feast our eyes in
half an hour with ten spectacles infinitely more
gorgeous than that which these men have gone
so far to see.   For *our* mountains change, sir.
They change.   The Cloud Artist (having the root
of the matter in him) never rests and says, "This
is good enough."   You say, "Ah, but the mountains change."   I admit it.   Within limits the
mountains do change.   But who, I ask you,
changes them ?   The Cloud Artist.

It is, I think, this Great Lovely Lucerne Joke
which makes the Cloud Artist so humorous on
days of cumulus.   While humanity is staring
fixedly at its own element he, aloft there, for his
own amusement, caricatures its treble-chinned
self-satisfaction.   And Earth, who knows her own
limitations, shares the jest at her children's
expense ; but, the while, like a good mother,
smiles indulgently on the loyal little things, and
spares no pains to make them happy.

XIII

OF A BLANK DAY

EVERY day of angling has some measure of joy and some of sorrow. There is, for example, the delight, always very keen, of viewing the water on arrival, though this has, within my experience, been wanting, the pond which I meditated fishing on one occasion having entirely disappeared, owing to a breach in its embankment. But this disappointment was balanced to some extent by the knowledge that I should never fish there again. It had been an infam— *nil nisi bonum*. On the other side of the account there is the sorrow of catching no fish. This is acute, and usual with me. But even on my blank days I can look back with pleasure. One carries away something with one from a river, though the creel be empty as the day it was woven. One cannot have failed to see all sorts of pretty things, to hear all sorts of pretty sounds, to smell sweet scents, to relish one's lunch. The senses have been exquisitely wooed. One has been out of London. That in itself is a rich satisfaction.

The blank day of yesterday was, considered as a day's fishing, particularly monotonous in its blankness. Between ten in the morning and nightfall my strained eyes may have witnessed perhaps three young grayling dimple the surface of that chalk stream, and once—tremendous moment!—a pike struck. But to a sportsman such as I was that day the doings of the fish were a small matter. Elsewhere than under water the items of my bag were found.

My scientific friend, Slattery, had given me a ticket for the White Water, three miles across the downs. His day's work ended, he was to come out by train for the evening, and we were to walk back together to Willows. I anticipated much pleasure from my day's angling, much from my walk home in the moonlight with Slattery.

Now you shall hear what happened.

From my arrival on the bank until midday, Hope—faithful creature—buoyed me stoutly up. Line greased, gut soaked, pale olive (I had seen one) attached, paraffined, wetted and dried, net ready on hip, I moved up the White Water at the regulation pace (when fish are not moving) of one quarter-mile in the hour. My eye scanned the surface, searched the depths. My ear was cocked for any likely little sound. I was craft incarnate. Towards noon this overwrought condition of my faculties (combined with a complete lack of any sign that the river held fish) produced its inevitable effect. My vigilance relaxed. The lustre of my purism became dimmed. I put on a large Wickham.

At the first cast a swift took it as it was falling. The force of habit struck—I am myself incapable of such an act—and after a short contest the misguided bird was brought to hand, unhooked, and returned to the air. The Wickham, dressed on a No. 1 hook, I have always found peculiarly deadly to swifts. This particular specimen, however, proved wholly innocuous to the trout, if trout there were.

Under such conditions luncheon is doubly welcome. One eats with no sense of time lost. One's enjoyment of food—a very proper enjoyment—is not marred by any anxiety about the river. One lingers over the cigarette that follows and the cigarette that follows it. One does not hurry. There are no fish anywhere at all. One dismisses fish from one's mind and takes one's pleasure in mastication, like a wise man. So I lunched. It was a good lunch, thoughtfully combined by a mistress of the art. There was marmalade in it and a pottle (I think it was a pottle) of ripe strawberries, also half a lobster, lettuce, many things. I have seldom had a better

lunch while fishing. At length, recollecting that
I was not here to guzzle (all was over with the
strawberries), but to catch a trout for my wife,
I lit tobacco and rose slowly to my feet. And
I perceived a duck's egg, pale green against the
darker grass—no shell-less wind egg—as honest
an effort as ever was dropped in haste and
collected at leisure. I was very much pleased
at finding this egg. My wife does not like duck's
eggs, but I do, and I get too few of them. I
ought to have more. They are a particularly
sustaining form of egg. I made a nest of sweet
hay for it in my creel, covered it up carefully,
and passed on, indescribably strengthened. I had
something in the creel.

During the next three hours I made slow but
steady progress up river, cheering my soul with
thoughts of the morrow's breakfast, soothing her
with contemplation of the landscape when the
water became unbearable. The beeches were
exquisite, sweet scents were everywhere, cuckoos
hooted, fieldfares piped, the Cloud Artist was
wonderfully inspired that day. I met an inspector
of the conservancy, who asked to see my licence.
I indulged his fancy. His obvious disappointment
was alone worth leaving Willows to see, not to
mention the shilling I had paid in the local post
office for that piece of paper. Wishing me good

sport in a bitterly resentful voice, he withdrew.
The spirit of a wish has never more signally been
fulfilled at the expense of its letter. Hope left
me by the water, admiring creation. Five o'clock
brought appetite and, appropriately, a little
public-house. I was half full of seed cake and
damson jam before I thought of my duck's egg.
But it would come in at breakfast. The charge
for tea was preposterously small. Well content,
I rejoined the river.

An hour passed, a delicious hour in which the
sun, creeping unwillingly to bed after his riot
among the clouds, threw out longer and longer
shadows under the trees, flushed the green downs
with rose, performed miracles—for me. For me
the birds sang loudly, praising the good weather.
The trout showed no interest in these things. I
gathered kingcups. While reaching for a particularly splendid bloom which grew low by the
water's edge, I was staggered to perceive a movement, a break in the surface among some rushes
some little way above me. Hope came fluttering
back. With the infinite precaution of a boy scout
engaged on his first practical demonstration of the
principles which he has imbibed from Major-
General Baden-Powell, I approached the site of
the unbelievable occurrence, and beheld, raised
from the water, as it were a bunch of feathers,

motionless, the stern of a bird which, head buried in weed, obviously supposed itself safe from observation. I felt almost certain that it was not an ostrich, though its manœuvre lent colour to that belief. To make absolutely sure, I stooped, and, taking a secure grip, extracted a waterhen— red bill, yellow legs, and all. I had never hitherto guddled a waterhen, and the experience was highly pleasurable. Having heard that these birds are succulent, I thought once of despatching the thing and placing it in my creel to keep the egg company; but it lay quite still in my hands, and its frightened eye disarmed me. Also a shrill little squeaking arose from amidst the rushes, and a small black ball with a scarlet neb became visible, oaring furiously away. This was the child of my captive. It caught sight of me and dived, swam six inches under water, rose, squeaked, dived again, and was no more seen. But its tender voice completed the work. If I destroyed its mother it must undoubtedly perish. Probably I was contemplating an infringement of the law— moorhens are just the sort of bird that would be protected. I restored my prey to the water. It dived, and reappeared presently, uttering maternal calls. I wandered on, my heart aglow with the consciousness of a skilful deed and a good action. All this time no sign of Slattery.

Dusk found me on the point of land which lay between the end of a mill-tail and the main river. A snipe was bleating about in a neighbouring meadow. There was a primrose sky above one down, a young moon above the other. A water-rat emerged from shadow and took its slanting course across the river, bent on some petty business or other. Idly I cast my line (by this time I was fishing a sedge, wet, down-stream) athwart its course, to see the furry thing dive, always a charming spectacle. It dived. I had hooked a water-rat.

A man approached on the other side of the mill-tail, and, thinking that I had a fish, congratulated me on my fortune. I perceived that he was Slattery. About the same time I drew a highly incensed water-rat on to the gravel at my feet. He was hooked lightly in the extreme point of the tail. As I lovingly unfastened the hook he turned, and with hideous ingratitude bit me to the bone of the first finger of my left hand. Then he rushed into the river. I uttered a loud cry. Slattery, supposing I had lost my fish, cried, " Hard lines ! " I said, " It's bitten me." " Bitten you ? " he repeated. " Bitten you, did you say ? " It occurred to me that I had not told him what I had been catching. If he believed it to have been a trout his surprise was very natural. "It was a rat," I mumbled, my finger in my mouth. "A rat?" he cried, and vanished. I thought him unsympathetic, thereby wronging him utterly. The blood gushed; I went up to the mill, my mind dark with misgivings. Blood poisoning, in my imagination, had already set in, and by the time I beheld the man of science hurrying towards me through the gloom my arm had been amputated. This extreme measure had failed, and they were measuring me for my coffin. Slattery carried a little thing like a slate pencil in his hand. He explained that it was a rod of lunar caustic, which, just before leaving his house that morning, he had found lying about and had slipped into his pocket. It was the first time he had ever carried such a thing with him. I swear that this happened.

Thus, with a sharp burning sensation, ended this eventful day. Fishing I had had none, but with a swift, a duck's egg, a waterhen, and a rat to my credit, I could not complain that I had lacked sport. We trudged home to Willows, I nursing my finger. At the gate my wife met me. "Any luck?" she inquired, with her usual hopeful smile. I felt in my creel for the egg. It was smashed. "Nothing," said I. "What!" she cried. "Not a single bite all day?" I was obliged to confess that I had had a bite.

Then I had reason to be grateful to the water-rat.

XIV

OF MacARTHUR, WITH A CONSIDERATION OF THE VAUNTED SUPERIORITY OF DRY-FLY FISHERMEN OVER WET-FLY FISHERMEN

I THINK I told you that I am not a Purist. Perhaps it is unnecessary to repeat it. But I want you to make no mistake. I fish by the dry-fly method because it suits my sluggish habits better than any other form of fly-fishing. But I claim no superiority for it over other methods. If I were not afraid of gentles I should no doubt be a roach-master, or something quite stationary like that. Now, sluggish though I am, my blood can mount at times. And, apropos of the dry-fly school, I feel it mounting now.

It is popularly supposed that dry-fly fishing is excessively difficult—difficult, I mean, beyond every other form of the art. I do not know who is responsible for this imposture. I imagine it must be the genius or genii who first applied the words "chuck and chance it" and "fine and far off" to the wet and dry methods respectively. I cannot think that any two epithets have ever

more successfully exalted one set of men at the
expense of another. You would suppose that any
fool can go and throw a blue upright into the
Barle at Dulverton and pull it out again with
a trout on it. You would imagine that no chalk-
stream fish may be lured at a less distance than
seventy yards.

Now there is no special merit in fishing with
a long line. No good fisherman, wet or dry, gives
a trout an inch more than is absolutely necessary.
Perhaps, of the two, the wet-fly man uses the
longer line, and he certainly, if he means to catch
fish, throws as "fine," by which I understand
"light," as the wet condition of his lure will let
him. But "fine and far off" remains the special
property of the dry-fly school, and the wet-fly
men continue to go about under the imputation
of "chucking it and chancing it." This shows
how important it is to be first in any field, even
of mutual recrimination. The arrogant dry-fly
school has fastened "chuck and chance it" on the
other fellows for ever, and nobody pays any
attention to their answering "creeping and
crawling" beyond stamping it vulgar and jealous
abuse.

This cheap sneer at the wet-fly man has proved
so successful that he himself has come to believe
that it is true. He forgets that his knowledge

of the trout's habits is much larger than that of his self-constituted superior. He forgets that if the two of them (grant me two fishermen of a sort of hypothetical, mathematically abstract character, each knowing nothing of his rival's methods) are placed on the banks of an unknown fast stream, that knowledge will enable him to give the dry-fly man first fishing over every pool and run, and that, after the dry-fly man has laboriously and vainly flogged every inch of the water, he (the wet-fly man) can come along and take a brace or more in a dozen casts, placed deftly in the twelve spots where, from the condition of the water, the state of the weather, the season of the year, and a hundred other things about which the dry-fly man knows nothing at all, he suspects the good fish are lying. He forgets similarly that, placed on the banks of an unknown chalk-stream, he and the dry-fly man are reduced to an equality in that a rise, breaking the surface of the water, speaks to both of them with the same sound, and that a fish lying in mid-stream is equally visible to both of them. He does not realise that a knowledge of the fishes' habits is (I speak comparatively) practically no part of a dry-fly angler's equipment. The mere fact that on a chalk-stream he can jettison the best part of the lore which it has taken him many years to acquire without doing his chances of sport any harm whatever, should cause the wet-fly man to think better of himself. But he does not know this. Again, he does not realise that the dry-fly man owes half his vaunted accuracy of casting to the rod-maker and the line-spinner, and that in this particular also they are pretty much on a level (it is understood again that I speak of the skilful of both schools). He does not realise that to be the dry-fly man's equal, if not superior, he has only to buy a certain kind of apparatus, to learn not to work his fly, to avoid drag, to pull in his slack and to distinguish between a number of unfamiliar artificial patterns—all matters surely within his competence.

No, he accepts the estimate which the world, taught by the dry-fly man, has formed of his attainments, and until he has tried a chalk-stream for himself, imagines that he might as well fish in his mother's pail as in the Test. He is all wrong, and here is an incident to encourage him.

In the early part of this century a man, whom I will call MacArthur, came upon me out of the East, demanding a chalk-stream and instruction in the dry-fly business. As he made it already understood that he was to pay for the chalk-stream, I undertook to introduce him to a water which I had fished during the five previous

seasons, and, because I was poor, had given up.
My anxiety to return to that water (for it was
this water), plus the deep affection 1 had for
MacArthur, blinded me to the second part of
his demand.

In the course of a few posts MacArthur was
the better by a rod for the season and I by twelve
guests' tickets. During those early days, while
we waited for May to come round, MacArthur's
confidence in and reverence for my knowledge
and skill were highly gratifying. He had never
used a dry fly, and although he had not his equal
as a wet-fly fisherman, he was filled with that fear
of the chalk-stream and that humbleness of spirit
of which I have spoken. He had looked upon
those who do their business in clear waters as
belonging to an order of beings higher altogether
than his own. He abased himself before me as
an initiate designate of some esoteric cult might
abase himself before its Grand Lama. He re-
ceived my lightest word on dry-fly angling as if
it were a revelation, and, without a word of com-
plaint, permitted me to spend many pounds of his
money on the purchase of a valuable rod, reel,
line, and other things. He said that if he were
permitted by Heaven's help and mine to slay one
trout out of that river before he returned into the
Orient, he would die blessing my name.

Nothing that I could say would persuade him
that chalk-stream fishing is pure skittles compared
with that he was accustomed to find in a tiny
bush-shrouded brook near Midhurst (a place in
which he could catch trout all day long while I
should have spent my time cutting down trees).
Nor could I get him to understand that, easy
though dry-fly fishing might be, I am extremely
unhandy at it. He said that I only talked like
that to encourage him, whereas I was really trying
to encourage myself. For I had discovered that I
possessed a reputation up to which nobody could
possibly live, and as the day approached when
I should have to " show him how to do it " at the
expense of those fish under whose contempt I had
writhed five summers long, I wondered sometimes
if I had not better perhaps break my right arm in
two places, and so preserve to MacArthur the last
ideal that he was ever likely to cherish.

At length the first day of May dawned, and my
right arm was still (as much as it had ever been)
at my service. I made, as the newspapers relate
of the condemned, a hearty breakfast of sausages
and bacon, and smoked a cigarette while Mac-
Arthur greased his line for the third time since
he had risen. Presently we were by the water's
edge, and for half an hour I showed MacArthur
how to cast his fly over imaginary fishes, and how

to keep his rod's point up and pull in the slack,
all of which he managed to do easily. You are
to remember always that MacArthur was a most
accomplished fisherman. Suddenly he found a
fish—which I had failed to observe. It lay near
the bank on which we stood, evidently just posted
for breakfast, about fifteen yards above us. The
water was clear of rushes and weeds, nor was
there any eddy or glide. The bank was free from
high grass and trees, and all other nuisances.
The wind blew gently up stream. I had a perfectly clear right-hand horizontal cast. It was
what is called a "sitter." As we looked, the fish
sucked down a fly.

"Have at him," said MacArthur, as he crouched
to the earth. (What he had not read about dry-
fly fishing was not worth writing.) "I want to
see just how you do it."

It was inconceivable that I should ever find
a more easily-placed trout. I knelt down, as the
books recommend, let out line, cast, and the wind
—the kindly wind of the west—dropped a pale
olive three inches above the nose of the fish, which
took it instantly. I hooked him, rattled him
down stream, and had him in the net before the
howl which MacArthur uttered as I struck had.
ceased to reverberate among the surrounding
chalk-hills. I do not hesitate to say that the

thing could not have been better done. I said,
" There ! "

MacArthur was breathing heavily through his
nose, and his eyes were shining with delight and
excitement and triumph. He had seen the luring
and slaughter of a chalk-stream trout—a trout of
1¾ lb., a trout twice as big as the biggest he had
ever looked on. He said that it was magnificent,
and launched into praises of my skill. I pre-
served a modest demeanour, and told him that
now he must get one. He despaired of ever
attaining to my accuracy and deadliness.

Seeing a fish rise about three hundred yards
up stream (he has an eye like a telescope), he
besought me to come and catch that one too,
as he had hardly had time to observe my methods.
He said it was a privilege to watch me. I did
not say what I would do until we reached the
rising fish, when I told MacArthur that he must
have a go at it. I pointed out that he had not
taken a rod on this river to watch me catching
fish, but to learn to do it himself. I insisted on
his trying for this fish.

The place in which it lay was situated twenty
yards across the stream, under the overhanging
branch of a willow, and on the far side of a thin
line of rushes and weeds. The rushes and the
branch were so disposed that the only possible

chance of getting a fly to the fish was to shoot it out of a gun through a gap some ten inches wide. I said, "This is not a particularly easy cast. But, remember, if you hook him you must bustle him. Though you break, you mustn't give him his head. This is your only chance. Recollect what I told you about raising your rod high in the air and walking backwards into the meadow? This is an occasion when you must do that."

MacArthur asked me if it was possible to cock a fly properly at that distance. This seemed to be the only doubt that troubled him. I told him (because he had on a dry, well-oiled and well-made fly, which would cock itself quite independently of the person who threw it) that it was quite possible.

"For you, perhaps," said MacArthur, and as he began to get out line I could feel the blushes chasing each other up and down my body. The next moment MacArthur's fly passed through the gap which I have described and lit, cocked to a miracle, in the only square inch of water where it could have served any useful purpose whatever. The trout hurled itself on to the hook. MacArthur struck, raised his rod high in the air, and began to walk backwards steadily into the meadow, just as I had told him to do.

The trout, paralysed with astonishment, followed obediently, wriggled itself bodily over the weeds and through the rushes, swung in the deep safe water for a second, and made off up stream like lightning. But he was well hooked, and there was never any cause for alarm. MacArthur reeled him in, let him run, reeled him in again, and after the usual fuss and bungling with the net, I got him to land—2¼ lb. MacArthur was dumb with delight. When I had recovered the power of speech, I said, " You now see how easy dry-fly fishing really is. Any man who can cast as you do may fish a chalk-stream with every prospect of success." I advised him to go up the river and practise on his own account. " All you have to do," I said, "is to avoid drag and pull in your slack, and forget that you ever thought there was anything difficult about this game."

The really remarkable feature of this story is that at the end of the day MacArthur admitted that the capture of his first trout was a fluke, whereas it was not. It was the masterly cast that did it. MacArthur, though he had never fished a chalk-stream, knew more about casting than nine dry-fly anglers out of ten that you will meet in conversation. But, though he brought back two other fishes, he had acquired a respect— a quite proper respect—for the many which he

H

had failed to take, and in the light of this experience he was inclined to belittle his first supreme performance. He was enchanted with his sport, but by no means puffed-up, and he was as ready as ever to sit at my feet and hear me talk, in spite of my having caught nothing more. Subsequently, during that season, he beat my take every time, and I think he must have modified his view of my dexterity. But he never let me see this, which shows, first, what a magnificent nature is MacArthur's, and, secondly, that a first-rate wet-fly angler who approaches a chalk-stream with the proper rod and line, and takes an instructor in whom he has implicit confidence, can do as well as anybody, if he will only follow that instructor's hints to the letter. But I have yet to hear of the dry-fly man who mastered wet-fly fishing in a season, or in five seasons. Two things are necessary to both arts: an apparatus and manual skill. But to the wet-fly game must be added knowledge. And the greatest of these is knowledge.

XV

OF CATCH-SINGING IN HIGH PLACES

UP on the downs the skylarks are not having it all their own way this summer.

I know three catches. One of these my wife knew previously to our marriage.

The other two I have taught to her. These we sing as we walk the hills of Wiltshire.

To the musically untutored there is something peculiarly intoxicating in the sound of their own voices. This characteristic of humanity has caused many good men who live in the vicinity of frequented high roads to blaspheme on their pillows. I am not a good man, but I have blasphemed like the best of them, and for the same reason, while the Lower Orders have been returning home of a Saturday or a Sunday night. I have often wished for a snipping instrument large enough to sever at one operation the vocal chords of all the musically untutored, forgetting that I am one of them. I am glad now that the opportunity was not granted to my impious prayer. For I should have done it, and I should now have been unable to sing on the downs. I hope that I shall for the future have a larger toleration for the musically untutored. But I fear that I shall not. A present desire for sleep will always prevail over the most pleasurable memory of vocalisation. I shall almost certainly blaspheme again.

The catches which we sing are the following : *Scotland's* (or *London's*) *Burning; A Boat, A Boat!* and *Frère Jacques.* The last is in French. When we render it we feel exorbitantly clever, for to sing at all, in harmony, places us among the artists, but to do it in a foreign tongue—this is culture.

To the musically untutored part-singing is an unattainable mystery, bellowing with the aid of a cornet in, as nearly as possible, unison being the summit of their ambition in this direction. But if they would only try a simple catch or two, they would find themselves executing what is admittedly one of man's most difficult feats—I mean harmonising their sounds with the sounds of other people. And they would feel like gods and never do anything else. But they know nothing of catches. The popular numbers of last year's pantomimes are all they can memorise. Now it is surely as easy to learn *Frère Jacques* (I dwell on this one with particular pride), which is unlike any other tune whatever, as it is to learn *Give my*

Regards to Leicester Square, which is undistinguishable save by three notes and a modulation (I speak as one of the musically untutored) from thirty other tunes of its class. And if they would take the trouble to master this simple little French air and attack it boldly one after the other they would be amply rewarded. They would discover that after a period of bawling, with ears shut as far as possible to everybody else's efforts, their own voice would be heard blending deliciously with the voices of other people, and, what is more remarkable, they would be able to maintain their striking performance indefinitely. They would catch themselves harmonising, and would step instantly from the ranks of sheer noise into the ordered realm of Art. And they would be purified and give their regards to Leicester Square no more. Therefore the People's Palace Musical Festival is a thing to send guineas to, though I do not myself do this.

We did not attain our present degree of perfection in catch-singing without a good deal of toil. Nothing really worth doing, except eating and drinking and sleep, can be learned easily. You will remember that I had to teach two of our numbers to my wife. This was a terrible business. It is one thing to sing a tune so that one recognises it oneself; it is another to give it out

so that some one else is able to recognise it. My
wife is far from being one of the musically untutored, but she was not sufficiently educated to·
pick up instruction from me. She had to work
at it, I promise you.

When I hummed *Frère Jacques* to her for the
hundredth time it was not her fault if she thought
I was occupied with *Scotland's* (or *London's*) *Burning.* But my resolution and her patience have
triumphed, Love (which is capable of all things)
co-operating; and now we never mix our tunes,
and our harmonies are blended in a manner entirely
satisfactory to ourselves.

This singing in the open air is a most uplifting
exercise. On the downs it is intoxicating. Where
no rabbit can move unobserved within earshot
one's freedom from human observation is complete.
Singing on a bicycle is also good, but, moving
rapidly between hedges, one is never sure that
some idiot child or shattered tramp has not been
left behind. But on hill-tops one is free of all
restraint in this kind, and one can pull out all
the stops.

Argument for the same reason is also carried
on with great luxury in these high places. But
argument is more dangerous because, once involved in a chain of reasoning (and how involved
one can become!), these unselfish considerations are

apt to vanish, and, caring nothing though all the children in England be rendered imbecile, one descends into regions of comparative civilisation in the full flood of roaring ratiocination. Chavender declared, during his visit, that whilst angling one afternoon blamelessly[1] by the river he imagined for a few moments that he had found a reason for his lack of success in distant thunder, which presently became articulate and recognisable as periods which pulverised the Specialisation of the Modern Actor. He was careful, I notice, to find out what his hostess had been discussing during the after-tea walk, and also, the slave! to elicit her views on the subject. Once assured that she favoured the special line of business, he no longer hesitated to imperil his soul in the manner I have indicated. Therefore that night he returned to an excessively large teapot.

But I digress unworthily.

Yet I find that I have said all that I have to say about our singing of catches.

---

[1] His own description of his proceedings.

XVI

OF FLOUNDER FISHING AS AN ART

TO the True Purist all things are pure. We are not all true purists. In every angler, however, the purist lurks. In one he is predominant, in another he is subordinate to the hunter. I confess that in me the hunter is the top dog. When I see a trout, for instance, a beast of prey rises within me and chokes the sportsman. I want to catch, not to fish. But when I see a bull-head the lust of slaughter is less fierce— I cannot say why—and I am ready to be an artist for art's sake. The fact is that I have not the skill to be a purist in trout-fishing, and I know that there are many anglers who are in like case. The object of that which follows is to indicate to these, my weaker brethren, a direction in which their better natures may perhaps find room for development. Let it be understood that I do not address the purist of the chalk-stream. That which follows is intended for those whose purity is equal only to the strain attendant upon the pursuit of flat-fish.   Lofty minds can find no food for thought here.

The capture of the flounder (*Pleuronectes flesus*) does not at first sight seem to offer much opportunity for the exercise of preciosity.   But it is possible that neolithic man regarded the trout itself as an article of diet rather than as a field for research, and where the flounder is concerned anglers are, generally speaking, in the same stage of civilisation as he.   Yet, if the best of us have learned to see *fario* as he is, may not the bunglers grope after a clearer vision of *flesus*.

With my friend MacAlister I was seated in the Arctic Circle on a sunny afternoon by the side of a certain sea-stream, the entrance, that is to say, and the exit of the Atlantic into and out of a tidal lake.   MacAlister had beaten the water cruelly until it had nearly all fled away into the sea.   I may add that he had caught nothing.   He had beaten the water, but the water had beaten him.   The sea-trout lay off the mouth of the sea-stream and laughed in their beards.   As for me, being clean-shaven, I laughed in my sleeve. MacAlister did not laugh at all.   There was no sport to be had.   We were, therefore, in a mood peculiarly suitable for the reception of the puristic seed when we were aware of Master Peer Gynt, who came delicately, on bare feet, over the pebbles and entered the water. In his hand he carried a little spear. This he drove through the body of a flounder, which he threw upon the bank, and again, and yet again. Here was a worthy sport indeed. But we had no spears.

Necessity is the mother of purism. The trout-fisher, having no worm, imagines the artificial fly. The flounder-fisher, having no spear, imagines the landing-net. To catch a flounder in a landing-net is not so easy as it sounds. To begin with, your flounder is a very fearful and crafty fish. He is so fearful that he has made himself exactly like the sand and weed on which he lives. It is therefore very difficult to find him, unless one has exceptional eyesight like Master Peer Gynt. He is so crafty, that when you disturb him by treading about in the water he flits imperceptibly to a new spot, where, with a single shiver of his body— a feat of *leger-de-corps* in which he has no equal —he covers himself with sand. His little horrid eyes alone remain visible, and these he fastens upon you with a cold stare, full of malevolence.

The first step in puristic flounder-fishing must now be taken, the hypnotism of the quarry. The practitioner will fix his eyes on those of the flounder, and will approach him cautiously from behind. On reaching the flounder he will lower his landing-net until it is upright in the water,

touching bottom a few inches in front of the
flounder's nose. This manœuvre can be executed
only if the angler maintains the hypnotic gaze.
If his eye wavers for an instant the flounder
will see the descent of the landing-net and dart
away. All being ready, the purist will advance
the right foot and tread heavily on the tail of the
flounder. The flounder will then dash into the
landing-net. This is the crude form of the sport.

MacAlister and I soon tired of such simple
work, and began to refine upon it. We allowed
the puristic part of our natures full play. We
raised flounder-fishing to the dignity of what it
is—an art. First of all we ruled out all spears,
baits, and hooks. These we left to Master Peer
Gynt and the pot-hunters. Then we made a law
that no flounder should be touched except on
clean sand. This was necessary, because Mac-
Alister had shown symptoms of wishing to take
his hands to them among the weed. The man
who would guddle *flesus* would be capable of any
infamy. Thirdly, we decided that any fish which
should bolt into the net before he should actually
be trodden on, should be considered "foul
started" and returned to the water. We fixed
a size limit—a two-and-threepenny French fire-
proof frying-pan. Then we made any but round-
mouthed landing nets unlawful and impure. A

V-shaped net, owing to the large space of sand which it straddles when inverted, gives the quarry little or no chance. We agreed that any fish which should evade the net once should be let alone, for after he has been driven from place to place for some time a flounder loses heart, and allows himself to be taken with ridiculous ease. Even a good sportsman will respect a gallant and skilful antagonist, and rejoice in his escape: but as purists we were actuated by a still higher principle. With the purist it is first time or not at all. The proper exercise of his skill is to him of such moment that one bungle disqualifies him in his own eyes from proceeding further in the matter.

I could fill many volumes with suggestions for the elevation of flounder-fishing; but a too elaborate exposition would defeat my object, which is not to instruct, but to set others in the way to learn. The truth is only to be found by patient personal search. The seeker, once his feet are set in the right path, must work out his own salvation. It is enough if I have shown him a means of purging his soul of some dross, of clearing some of the mud from his waders. I have offered him one or two stepping-stones. For the rest of the journey across the gulf let him trust to his own higher nature—not to mine.

XVII

OF LESS CONSEQUENCE

CONCERNING a wonderful little study of a pollard willow which I sent him the other day, the professional painter writes this: "I don't recommend perfectly round trees. For composition's sake, break off at least one bough."

A hatchet, then, is an essential part of a landscape painter's equipment; but as I do not find it included in my catalogue, which is certainly very complete, it may be that there is some explanation of this hint which has escaped me. And Farmer Lavender would object. I know he would. Until I can communicate with my master I will leave perfectly round trees alone.

.   .   .   .

After search I find that there are no perfectly round trees in this valley. I am therefore relieved of the necessity of injuring Mr. Lavender's pollards. I rejoice. But this shows how careful my master is. He knows the danger of the circular tree to young painters. I am in good hands.

.   .   .   .   .   .

In his letters my master continually refers me to the work of Turner. For example, he says : " All methods of handling are legitimate—provided they come off. Turner used thousands." This is very encouraging. If Turner used thousands there seems to be a good chance that mine is one of those which this great painter used. If it were so, how fine it would be !

.   .   .   .   .   .

A man has been here. He is only a black-and-white artist, and is a little jealous, naturally, that I should handle a superior medium. He has looked at some of my little things. He said: " Your method seems to me to be——" I did not wait to hear the adjective. I said: " All methods are legitimate—if they come off." He said : " I grant that, on those terms, yours may be admirable. Bring me a wet sponge and let us see." I was glad when he went away, because I hate to rouse any man's envy. Yet I was sorry, for on all other counts I love him.

Everybody who sees my pictures—that is to say, everybody who comes inside our garden gate—admires them immensely. It is extraordinary that in a little village like Willows there should be so many good judges of art. Our laundress, now, Mrs. Stiggins—she thinks the world of them. A fig for that fellow!

.   .   .   .   .   .

I now paint freely about in the village. Nobody bothers me, as I feared they would. Perhaps, out of sheer courtesy, they come and look over my shoulder. But they never stay long. I think they fear to intrude.

.   .   .   .   .   .

I have given one of my pictures to Mrs. Stiggins. Signed. It is a picture of her pretty cottage. She came and watched me as I painted it, and I gave it to her.

.   .   .   .   .   .

My picture of Mrs. Stiggins's cottage is hung—nailed, I should say. I have seen it in Mrs. Stiggins's parlour. On one side is the almanac of a friendly society. On the other is a large shell with a view of Bournemouth Pier inside it.

My picture is easily the best, regarded purely as a work of art. Mrs. Stiggins's brother was in the cottage when I called about a collar that was missing from last week's wash. He lives opposite to Mrs. Stiggins. He asked me if this might be one of the houses hereabouts. I believe him to be a trout-poacher, and I am sure that that was my collar which I saw round his neck.

.   .   .   .   .   .

Since I gave the picture to Mrs. Stiggins nobody has looked over my shoulder while I have been working. I expect they think that it would look like hinting.

.   .   .   .   .   .

When I come in from painting luncheon has been ready for some minutes. Any other woman would complain, but my wife does not. She is too anxious to see my picture. She has a very keen eye for the virtues of my work, and I never go wholly lacking a word of praise. It is comforting, as I wrestle, sometimes rather hopelessly, with the problems which I set myself, to know that the result is sure of a kind reception. The interest she takes in them doubles the joy of my labours. I am very like a child making mud pies and bringing them to its mother for approval. We both know that my paintings are abominable, but she pretends that they are exquisite, and we lose ourselves in admiration while the soup gets cold.

XVIII

OF THE CRACKLING OF THORNS

SOMETIMES, as I walk on the valley road on my way to or from the water, a waggonette containing a party of pleasure meets or passes me. I always have the feeling that the incident has sensibly enlivened the journey for these people. Did they seem bored? Smiles appear. Were they hilarious? The downs reverberate with their cachinnations. Mirth in itself is good; therefore I like to hear these people laugh, to see them smile. But mirth of that particular quality is not good. Its other name is derision; it is the child of ignorance, and ignorance is begotten of the pit. Therefore I weep that I should be the cause of stumbling to these poor souls. But what am I to do?

I know that my costume and equipment are to blame, and they alone. In myself I am not a ludicrous-looking man. My features are no more out of drawing than those of ninety-nine in a hundred. I am no *homme qui rit*. If you saw me in my everyday clothes you would never dream of thinking me a comical object; you would not notice me at all. I am quite inconspicuous as a general rule, but when I go fishing these painful demonstrations greet me from everyone not fortunate enough to dwell beside a chalk-stream. It can only be my rig. But what, I repeat, am I to do? I believe that I may look a little more out of the way than some other anglers. At no time am I a dapper man, and with the large excuses which the craft affords me, a native carelessness slides easily into that wholehearted lack of decorum which is best observed emergent from a field of ripe grain. I wear my oldest clothes, and how old they are it is now quite impossible to say, but they are delicious to my body, and barbed wire can do them no harm whatever. I have seen natty anglers, men in new clothes with waders that fitted them like skin, brogues that would have done credit to any lady's drawing-room, snowy linen, jewellery, buttonholes —one even with his oil bottle in a little bag of chamois leather, as if it had been a watch fresh home from the makers. I have dubbed them carpet-fishermen, but in my heart I knew that they—some of them, most of them—killed more fish than I. The unconventional attire in which the American humorous artist loves to dress his

Weary Willies is not, then, an essential feature of the good fisherman, but there is no doubt that these exquisites are not common objects of the river bank. There seems to be some subtle relation between ancient clothes and angling, for, though I may go to extremes, I resemble far more the composite which would be obtained by photographing any dozen of anglers than do those immaculate sportsmen. As a class we are uncareful of our appearance, preferring comfort and freedom from anxiety to the neatest exterior, and as a class we suffer accordingly—but do not suffer from—the flouts of the uninstructed.

My own experience, then, is probably typical, and our fraternity is derided, which is not as it should be. Now, like all anglers who do their business in water-meadows, I must needs wear waders, or a rheumatic old age awaits me. Gum boots would be a concession to waggonette prejudices, but gum boots were invented by the devil as a special counterblast to the Second Commandment, and the devil does quite well enough as it is. Waders involve big socks, and big socks can only be worn inside brogues. The result is lumbering, but, after all, gum boots, even if one conceded, are only a shade less bulky. A broad-brimmed hat, again, is essential to comfort in bright as in rainy weather. A stream can only

be scanned successfully in a broad-brimmed hat.
The brim can hardly be too broad; mine might
have been sired by an umbrella. But when I
carry an umbrella (my hat is not nearly so large,
of course, as an umbrella) nobody sniggers,
nobody calls, "Come out, I can see your feet!"
Yet this admonition is commonly offered me by
the waggonetteers. This hat, like the hats of
other fishermen, is almost covered with flies; but
where else am I to put my flies to dry, now that
the front of my fishing coat has no more room
for them? Honestly, I can think of no other
place which would be at all convenient. I have
a few in my trousers, but they got there un-
intentionally, and when I am fishing they are
quite inaccessible. I have no reason to think
the trousers a good place for carrying flies. And
if a broad-brimmed hat covered with feathers and
fur is a risible object, what gaiety should reign
in Regent Street during shopping hours! But
I have never noticed any excess of it thereabouts
at those times. To give an instance of the sort
of thing my hat causes otherwise decent people
to say, a man once told me that I looked like a
boomfood mushroom that had gone into the catch-
'em-alive-o business. But what, I ask, am I to
do? Must I suffer agonies from sunburn and eye-
strain that malice may have no vent? I think not.

Waders—to touch for a moment upon another thing which characterises me only when prepared to angle—induce a certain deliberation of movement. Thus I have been addressed from behind as " old cockalorum " by a cyclist, who passed on his way with a hideous guffaw. The appearance of age, then, is funny. I suppose it is the board schools again. But time was when young Englishmen would not have cackled at the mere simulacrum of venerableness, for I am hardly middle-aged.

So, an object of ridicule, I make my rare encounters with the great intelligent world which lies beyond the bend in the valley (where the main line runs) and comes waggonetting it through my Elysium with a sneer for its cloddish rustics and a cat-call for old cockalorum. But how do these same cloddish rustics greet this side-splitting apparition that is William Caine? Do bucolic hee-haws burst from their large amiable mouths when we meet on the road? Does Sewsan lean shaking on the shoulder of Giles, Hodge, the while, rolling in agonies of mirth beneath the hawthorn? Not so. These folk, though they have never trod Cheapside, have knowledge that does not grow in cities. They are wise in their way—and foolish, doubtless, in their way; but their folly is not a discourteous folly, and their wisdom tells them that the things which they do not understand are not necessarily to be derided. And this is a good wisdom.

I find that I have worked myself into something like a heat over this matter of the non-angler's attitude towards fishing costumes. This was not my intention. I am casting stones at a host of good people — kind fathers, devoted mothers, excellent sons, brothers, daughters, sisters, self-denying aunts, bland, tip-bestowing uncles. Because they snigger at an undoubtedly bizarre get-up they are not therefore by me to be censured, for I have done the same. I have been tickled in my time by a golfer's red jacket, but that was before I learned the reason for it. Had I known—as I know now—that it was worn as a danger signal to persons who stroll on links that they may keep out of earshot of the players, had I known this I should have recognised the worth of the coat, and my eyes would have been blind to its comicality. Ignorance lay at the root of my amusement.

In the hope, then, of clearing away a cloud or two from the perception of a few fellow-beings I have written what I have written. I do not hope for much result from my toil, but he is a coward who spares himself trouble on so shabby an excuse. And it may be that someone in some future waggonette shall have read this little plaint, and the general merriment shall, by his, be lessened, the general ignorance by him be illuminated. And so—for, fair play to the cockney, he is receptive of ideas—the good seed shall bear fruit, and a day may come when a bean-feast descended from these honest citizens shall see in my grandson, as he goes on his way to fish for the trout which I now put down, not a harmless lunatic, fit target for waggery, but a decent angler, suitably clothed, and shall cry with one voice, not "Get your hair cut!" but "Tight lines!"

XIX

OF ANGLING TROPHIES

MUTUAL confidence being the foundation of society, we look askance at the liar as at an enemy of the human race. There is, moreover, no pleasure in lying for its own sake. A lie that takes nobody in becomes to its inventor "a dead sea fruit that turns to ashes on the lips." If he be not rewarded by the open-eyed admiration of his audience he had better have remained silent—yea, though he has lied like Ananias. For these two reasons we all wish to be believed, and it is a pitiful circumstance that the more untruthful we are the greater is our hunger for credence. The unimaginative man, who has nothing worth telling, need not and does not concern himself about the acceptance of his paltry stories. But the genius who has struck out a first-rate figment is touched in his being if the child of his fancy fails to make good.

Among anglers, therefore, a convention exists that everything shall be believed. In communities

where all men go armed courtesy and toleration
flourish, because no one knows what widespread
carnage may result from one over-hasty pistol-shot.
So fishermen, when they exchange their experiences, are careful to raise no eyebrow, to utter no
dubious cough, lest the gentleness which characterises the craft should suddenly give place to
wrath and contention. As of the whole, so of the
part. Mutual confidence is the foundation of our
society. We proceed upon the principle of "a lie
for a lie and an untruth for an untruth," all goes
swimmingly, and harmony prevails.

I can never understand why anybody should
have wished to improve upon this admirable state
of things. Yet, at one time or another, some
angler must have found it unsatisfying. He was
probably a fisherman of so prodigious a talent
that he found that he had achieved the impossible
by stretching too far the forbearance of his friends.
And so, to bolster up his position amongst them,
he went away and made a trophy. Armed with
some distorted effigy of a 10-lb. trout, he returned
to their midst and laid it before them in silence
—the proud, hurt silence of the deeply-wronged
man. Instead of tearing the traitor in pieces and
pulverising his cast, burning the fragments and
sowing the barren seashore with the ashes, they
gazed dumbly upon this proof of his veracity,

bowed low before him, and departed severally in search of plaster-of-Paris. A new era had dawned for anglers. Since that day in order to be a great fisherman it has been necessary to hang great casts on the wall.

Now if a man shows me a fish—a large dead fish —which he takes from his creel at the end of the day, I am prepared to hold it a convincing proof of his skill. I do not know how he came by it. I do not know if it was caught on a dry olive or with a worm or with a stroke-hall, whatever that may be. He may have bought it from a boy. He may have charmed it out to him on the bank with the music of the flageolet for all I care. I do not ask these things. He has a fish. I can handle it and recognise it for a fish by its touch and its appearance and its fishy smell, or, if it be a grayling, by its delicious odour of wild thyme. I am content. If his fish is bigger than any of mine, I tell him of one much bigger than his which broke me just after I began in the morning, when my gut was not thoroughly soaked. Yet I own frankly that he is an angler and I take off my hat to him.

But a plaster cast is a different affair. On its evidence I would rather hang its owner than yield him a tittle of respect. A plaster cast represents to me nothing but so much coin expended. If I had enough money I could have a cast as big as

the whale that swallowed Jonah. And I would.
If the house did not contain it, it should stand in
the garden and I would paint it once every three
years with not less than three coats of good and
substantial oil colour.

It was one of the greatest living anglers who
unwittingly opened my eyes to the fact that these
things are impostures. Wishing to impress me
with a proper understanding of his supremacy and
the length of time he had enjoyed it, he once told
me that the trophies of Thames jack which he
had collected during his residence at Oxford—at
Oxford, mark you, when he was a mere boy—were
so large that he could not afford to take them
down with him. He wished me, I believe, to infer
from this that the loss of his unique collection was
of less moment to him, the skilful angler, than
was the cost of its freight to Paddington to him,
the undergraduate, with many calls upon his purse.
But I gathered more from his abandonment of
these trophies than he perhaps intended me to do.
It is obvious that they were so big that they could
not be taken out of his lodgings without injury
to the house, and that the ground landlord obtained
an injunction against their removal as being parcel
of the freehold. To this inference a corollary
attaches. As they could not be taken out they
were never brought in. In other words, they were

made on the premises, and point to their creator's inordinate passion for fame a great deal more surely than to his success with the rod.

If a man should go into a court of law and swear that such and such a thing happened at half-past one by his watch, and should produce the very watch in proof of his statement, he would surely advance his case very little. Yet I have seen men stand in front of the counterfeit presentment of a trout so vast that, in the good old days before trophies were introduced, not a man among us would have dared to whisper its alleged weight—and swallow it, glass case and inscription, without an effort.

But the most pernicious feature of the trophy remains to be exposed. Unless an angler has casts to show he is looked upon with suspicion. I may expend treasures of ingenuity in adorning the relation of my exploits, but in the presence of my bare walls, my friends say, "We see that you do not care to have your fish set up. Some people don't." There are persons, of course, who cut their fish out of brown paper, and for some years after this method of angling was discovered it enjoyed a considerable popularity among the indigent. But for one reason or another—a brown-paper shape is not convincing. The most credulous eye sees through it. I suppose it is too easy to make, brown paper is too cheap; the thing has been overdone.   Besides, it does not look at all like a fish.   It has not the glass eye of the cast. It is flat, and though you colour it in chalk, it can never compete with the modelling and paint of the more expensive kind of trophy.   No, one looks down one's nose, now, at brown-paper fishes. They are thoroughly discredited.   The worst angler dare no longer hope for help from them. I have not made one for years.   As in every walk of life, there is in angling one law for the rich and another for the poor.   It is very hard.

XX

OF AN ASS

MY wife has discovered a little steed for us. He is called Jack, which is just as it should be, because his second name is Ass, and he is a sort of honorary member of the Bunting family— close neighbours of ours. Among beasts of draught this ass is surely one of the highly fortunate. He lives a life which has hitherto been lived only by the horses of sporting fiction. Roland, who carried a certain prosy-poetic, indomitable fellow from Ghent to Aix or from Aix to Ghent, may have been allowed in recognition of his services to spend thus the evening of his days. And in the last chapter of *The Starting Gate* we shall certainly find the dear old Druid cropping the lush grass of the Manor paddock or accepting sugar from the dainty hand of his mistress while the Squire stands by and recounts for the seventeen-hundredth time the story of the noble brute's last race, when, lame in the near hind, he won the Cup for his owner, together with a huge sum in bets, whereby he, the Squire, was able to marry and reform and save a great name from dishonour and the timber from the Jews. Never again has he, the Squire, run a horse. The stable was sold, but the Druid remained. Him the Squire would not let go. No, by Gad! He has earned an easy old age, the Druid has, and the Squire is seeing that he gets it. Yes, by Gad! A bulging grandchild is placed on the back of the old horse. He lumbers on three legs round the paddock and the book closes.

Yes, the horses of fiction live like Jack, but Jack is an ass of fact, and no ass, even of fiction, has ever before had so ideal an existence. A champion Pekingese could hardly fare better. The meadow in which he passes his days is full of long, sweet grasses; it is admirably shaded by elms. The sun shall not smite him by day unless it is his pleasure. The high road runs hard by. People walk there constantly, and they all pass the time of day with Jack. Most of them he ignores, but with a few, whom he favours because they bring gifts, he engages in brief conversation. The gifts displayed, accepted, and swallowed, he drifts away, which is his method of suggesting departure to his visitors. And let them go or stay, he gives them no more of his

attention. Except for these short excursions to
the fence he never stops eating. Now it is one
thing to have unlimited food, it is another to have
an unlimited appetite. I have heard the million-
aire pitied because, having the means to gratify
his taste for fine dishes to any extent, he is
physically incapable of eating more than one
dinner in the day. Therefore, it is argued, he
is really no better off than a much poorer man.
Jack is outside this kind of consideration altogether. Truly, he eats but one dinner a day.
But it begins in early morning, and it only stops
when he is led reluctantly stablewards at night.
He is like the cigarette-smoker, whose pleasure
consists enormously in the smoke itself, but
infinitely more in the not being without it. So
long as Jack is permitted to chew, so long he
remains contented, easy-tempered, placid. But
remove him from his victuals and he rapidly
grows irritable.

Until we came into the Valley such was the
ideal existence of this ass. Once a week, on
market day, Mrs. Bunting harnessed him to his
little cart and permitted him to trot into the town
with her and back. It was a jaunt that he enjoyed. Every creature above the limpet feels
now and then the need of a little gentle exercise.
This causes a quicker movement of the blood,

K

and the digestive system is benefited. To the grass-eater it is the tonic appetiser which his meals are to the cigarette-smoker. Even this, you see, was provided for the thrice and four times happy ass. The road to market is a pleasant road of an easy length, not hilly, passing among trees. Jack liked very well to jog his four miles there in his fifty minutes and to return in his forty-five. It set him up for the week, and it gave him that feeling of usefulness which, in however modified a form—Charity *Matinées* let us say, and most subscription dances—is necessary to perfect contentment.

But now—his hire is but a shilling—now he lives in a sort of Purgatory, not quite Hell. Any afternoon he may see Mrs. Bunting at the gate, and at the sight his heart dies within him. He knows what this portends. Whereas the really charming spectacle of Mrs. Bunting at the gate was wont to arouse within him the happy antici-pation of gentle movement not over-prolonged, for which his week's repose had absolutely inclined him; whereas the hebdomadary frolic was but a pleasant break in a monotony, rendered by it doubly delicious; whereas his legs carried him joyously to meet Mrs. Bunting, and he wore his shafts as a man wears his holiday suit, now he lowers his ears, ignores Mrs. Bunting, and tears sullenly at his pasture, as that same man (supposing him to be a trout fisher), with thought of the office waiting for him on the morrow, casts his fly doggedly into the last flicker of sunset. The shadow of work is darker than all the shades of night and blacks out the day long before the sun has gone down. But if any pleasure may be extracted from casting he means to have it. So Jack. But the succulent herbs are bitter in his mouth, and his face looks like a coffin.

For my wife has said to me in the morning, "Suppose we take the donkey to-day and go up on the downs." Notice this mode of expression. If it reflected the true state of the case I swear Jack would be delighted—but it does not. We do not take the donkey. The donkey takes us, and between the two there is a world of difference. The downs in question rise to a considerable height above the river-level. They are reached by hot, treeless roads, gentle in gradient but intolerably long. No pleasant constitutional for Jack, this down-climbing, but work, work that makes him sweat—even to think of it. Nothing could be better for his general health. He ought to be grateful to us. But is he? He may be, but he doesn't look it when he stands by the garden gate, his ears anywhere, his tail tucked between his legs. At every bump, which tells of some further article added to his load, his depression becomes more obvious. For on these journeys we require—

Grandmama, our tea-basket.

A parcel of provisions.

The Rookee chair.

Several books.

The shameless, leg-displaying umbrella, which we call the parasol.

Letter paper, in case my wife should wish to write letters.

Sermon paper, in case I should wish to write a book.

The implements of landscape-painting in water-colours.

Two cushions.

Two rugs.

A bottle filled with water.

A mackintosh, and

Each other.

Jack, on the contrary, has no conceivable use for any of these properties or persons, except, perhaps, the parcel of provisions. It is the thought of this which alone, I believe, keeps him from falling down on the road in despair (so sustaining are our provisions), for he knows that he will get his share. A miserable share—that is his opinion of it—and not in the least worth the

incredible labour that he has to perform to get
it, but—well, after all, marmalade between brown
bread and butter does not come along every day.
Yes, these excursions have their better side.
So by the time we are finally disposed in the rear
corners of the toy vehicle, he has very likely
brisked up, and on the principle that the sooner
the pill is swallowed the sooner the jam is got, he
generally sets off at a brisk pace.

This he maintains for one hundred yards.

Then he comes to the gate of his paddock, and,
throwing aside his virtues, makes one short but
determined effort to take us to tea on the other
side of our own party fence. I frustrate this—
for I am an accomplished club ("club" as a
synonym for the ass-driver is better because more
true than "whip"), and I know his habits. All
this involves a certain amount of pulling on one
rein, which he regards as a signal to halt. This
he does. I speak softly to him—we are in the
middle of the village; and my blood has not yet
begun to mount—urging him forward. So he
walks at funeral pace past his dear gate, and
having buried his hope yet once again, takes the
next quarter-mile with a great deal of unnecessary
action. Fixing one's eyes steadily upon him and
ignoring all other things, one would suppose that
one was racing over the road. Glance at the

hedge, and one discovers that the cart is just not standing still. For in the ingenious art of sugaring Jack is second to none. I assure myself that the club is in the cart, but I do not so much as finger it, for it is a principle with me never to belabour this poor dumb brute until I am well away from the chance of observation. On the downs, however, it is different. There the eyes of my wife and my Maker alone see what I do to this ass, and I have no fear. The one is in the same cart as I. The Other is able to judge between me and this ass, and I have absolute confidence of acquittal. But the hasty misconception of the ignorant I fear. My name would look well in a brutality case. In human justice I place no trust, but in that of Divinity I do absolutely confide.

There is a spot somewhere on the ass which by repeated blows I have rendered less callous than other parts of him. Sometimes I find it, and the ass seems to start in his sleep. Thus we gain a yard.

We have gravely discussed the use upon the ass of devices whose fiendish ingenuity and cruelty make me blush for the brains which could imagine them. I cannot write them down.

A hair-pin—I snatched it out—has almost been employed. But the hand of Mercy snatched it back. "It is the only one that I have which will stay in five minutes," said Mercy.

And I walk up all the hills.

And I really love the ass. He has an adorable nose.

On hills I find that a certain form of address is perhaps less useless with the ass than any other stimulus. It is necessary to imagine oneself a member of the criminal classes, to assume a vile, raucous, but muffled utterance, and to take words upon one's lips which no gentleman could possibly use. It is not necessary to articulate these words distinctly, thank Heaven! But though they be dissembled under mouthings, the intention to utter them must be there, and the criminal mind must be assumed as far as possible. This machinery, set going, produces such intimidating sounds that I have seen my wife shrink from me involuntarily, though she knows my golden nature to its core; as for the ass, they have driven him once as much as fifty paces at over four miles an hour.

To pull on the bridle as one walks up hill by the ass's side is madness. He believes that you are trying to pull him up the hill. And he lets you.

So time ends, eternity has grown very old, and we reach the summit and our picnic ground.

Here we tether the ass, and my wife busies herself with kettle and methylated spirit. While we have been approaching my eye has been concerned with the natural features of the position, and very likely I have already selected the tree, group of whins, haystack, or what not which is this afternoon to acquire immortality. Or my mood may be a large one, which nothing less than square leagues of the countryside can satisfy. In this case I stand awhile considering the great spaces that surround me. But soon my mind is made up. Where all is impossible, why waste time in seeking for the less among the more difficult? Have at it! The Ignorant nothing can intimidate. So, after a brief period passed in framing pictures between my two hands held sideways, I fix on a county or two and begin.

Great views make many people feel like worms and insects. As a corrective to this uncomfortable sensation let me recommend them to paint these vistas. Their delight in what they see will be in nowise diminished, nay, rather increased five hundred-fold, but their estimation of their own place in nature will rise. They will learn that it is not the part of a worm and an insect to capture and set down on paper any fractional percentage of this world's beauty. A worm's appreciation, for instance, of the view from Montreux up the

Rhone valley must be so small as to be entirely negligible. An ant's capacity to draw anything which remotely recalls Loch Assynt is nil. Handy little things though ants have been shown by scientists to be, they have never been found painting landscapes ; not by the highest-powered microscope. Men do this. Let these humble-minded people, therefore, thank Heaven that they are men, and if they fear to paint, let them revel in the power to paint and in the power to enjoy. But let us have no more talk of worms and insects. Though I paint the most horrible pictures from which the most kindly connoisseur turns fainting away, this distressing circumstance cannot rob me of my achievement. Perhaps it may be said that no one would wish to rob me of it. That it is worth nothing, nothing at all. This is sheer commercialism. I cannot get sixpence for all my pictures put together. Granted. But I have got from them what no amount of money could buy me. I have learned my superiority to the worms, a matter about which in my youth I had some very uncomfortable doubts. I know that I have faculties which raise me above worms, and I have exercised one of those faculties as honestly as I can. This is a great deal.

Again, let these people, when they paint, paint on smallish Whatman boards. To produce a sort of illusion of so much of the Universe on so small a space is to taste omnipotence. While one part of the soul prostrates itself before valley and wood, rolling down-land and the miracle of the clouds, another part sings loudly and contentedly while the daubing goes on. The child that is in us all plays happily at being father. We are engaged on the sincerest form of—not flattery, but worship. A lick of Burnt Sienna and a whole autumn forest, twenty miles away, is there, under our hand. Four thousand leaves lie in a brushful of Terre Verte, the infinity of space in a thin wash of Cobalt. A pool of Yellow Ochre, a dab of Vandyke Brown, and we own a thatched cottage. With a streak of Dragon's-blood we take seisin of territories. We play at Creation, and it is the best game (in all its forms) yet invented. And the real Artist smiles on our play.

But this nonsense of painting makes me neglect the ass, and neglect he detests. Of what his opinion of us may be I have, of course, no certain idea, but I cannot think that it is high. One of us he sees fiddling with an apparatus or seated immovable with a little book in her hand or strolling the down with hair flying loose upon the breeze shouting words of no meaning; the other squats on the ground making dirty a piece of white paper. Thus—or somewhat thus—he must

regard our recreations. And we give him no
sort of attention. Poor beast! He cannot recognise the preparation of tea and the acquirement
of a Spanish vocabulary, nor yet the production
of lovely pictures, when these phenomena present
themselves to his notice. To him they are as the
weaving of sand-ropes. (And who shall say that
he is wrong?) Boredom unspeakable descends
upon him. He surely hates us. At one point
only our proceedings acquire a certain interest
in his sight. It is when my wife gives him food.
I have referred to marmalade sandwiches. But
this is not the tale of his luxuries. Plum-cake
he knows, and sugar and macaroons and cucumber
and radishes. Gingerbread, too, he accepts. But
we enjoy his gingerbread more than he, for its
stickiness wraps it round his bit, and for long his
tongue explores for outlying portions. Since the
discovery of this entertainment we carry gingerbread always. Besides brown bread, he also eats
brown-paper and tissue-paper and string. And
he would once have eaten Oxide of Chromium,
but I rescued the tube. And there was a camp-
stool which we could never find. But perhaps
I insinuate an injustice. Let it stand. He has
more on his conscience than a camp-stool. For
at half-past five he begins to bray. It is the signal
for departure, and we depart, not because we wish

it, but because the ass wishes it. On our first
excursion to the downs he behaved himself most
seemly. "This," he thought, "is only once in
a lifetime. I can stick it out, for hang it! they
have given me lettuces." But the second time
was too much for the small spark of gratitude
and decency which then lurked in the black soul
of this beast. It went out. "This," he thought,
"is getting a bit too tough altogether. Confound
them and their *pâté de foie gras!*" And he lifted
up his voice in protest. The sacred peace of our
hill-tops was shattered by outrageous sounds.
The song of the ass is above nightingales in
one respect. It absolutely ensures attention. A
shocked world stopped to listen, laying aside its
business of rolling, and we—we went home, lest
the solar system be disorganised. I prayed to the
ass; I appealed to his better nature. He had
none. I appealed to his hide—the *argumentum
ad baculum.* He only made more and horrider
sounds. The study of Spanish was suspended.
A vigorous impression of Scotch pines was lost
to the world. What did the ass care? Nothing.
He was going back to paddock.

Since that afternoon he has always given the
signal for return. I am only surprised that he
does not do it before we leave Willows. But let
him try it. I would lather him braying through

the Three Villages. Half-past five, then, is his hour for "taking" us home. I think that two causes co-operate here—(1) he has rested himself sufficiently ; (2) he has removed the last layer of gingerbread from his bit. You suggest, acutely enough, more gingerbread. Our intelligence has risen so high. But a ton of gingerbread should not stop the ass's braying when he means to depart. He accepts the gingerbread, but he brays as he munches. So we return at a brisk pace, broken only at one spot, a public-house, up to which he always dashes at the gallop—and stops. For gingerbread is thirsty stuff. Behind him as we go, we sing, versifying alternately like troubadours, extolling his and our own merits, praising the institution of tea in the open, lampooning the Vicar, congratulating the Cloud Artist on the afternoon's arrangements.

At his paddock the ass makes one last determined bid for freedom, fails to bring it off, and ultimately, with a most righteous demeanour, trots the few remaining yards and draws up of his own accord at our gate. Mrs. Bunting appears labouring towards us, smiling to see the ass safely home. We unship our monstrous collection of necessaries. We all separate.

Five minutes later the ass has resumed his interrupted day's meal.

XXI

OF PATIENCE, AS IT TOUCHES ANGLERS

ALL this week I have been fishing for a large trout which lives—he still lives—hereabouts. He has just gone away, as he always does sooner or later.

The only thing that I can find to say in favour of this fish is that he has chosen for his dwelling a part of the river which I so greatly love.

In those far-off days when I was competent to catch trout, I have daped some woundy ones out of this narrow, shallow, jungly backwater. Here Chavender takes them freely. It is the overflow from many hatches up river. Where it begins who shall say? Its origin is lost in water-meadows, but it is fishable to the first drop. In a morning I have scared, not caught, a round dozen of two-pound trout in this inconsiderable runlet. On the hot still afternoons when the main river is hopeless as Avernus, here the fat yellow things swim slowly in the cool shade up and down, up and down, each on his own beat, sucking in the insects which fall from the roof of trees.

I love to see my fish. The unseen may be a monster (there is always that glorious uncertainty). She is more likely one of these little graylings, and your time has been utterly lost. But the sight of a three-pounder coasting a still pool is in itself an inspiration, and he provides just as much of glorious uncertainty as the smallest ring ever made by invisible fish. Therefore, I particularly haunt this shadowed place which is the best on the river. Here Purfling never comes. Such angling as one does here is, in Purfling's eyes, poacher's work, devil's work.

Here, then, I can avoid Purfling, and exercise that patience which is supposed to be an essential part of the angler's equipment.

In the days when I used to dine out, I always found that the lady who had the misfortune to go in with me knew—though we might be total strangers to one another—that I fished. It was usually the salmon or the filleted sole or the turbot (no other fishes are served at dinner parties) which suggested the observation, " I think you fish." The stranger we were to one another, the sooner this uncanny knowledge was manifested. I often pondered the mystery. I examined myself to see if angling had left some mark which these sharp-sighted creatures recognised. I wondered if my hands gave me away, if the wielding of the rod had moulded my right hand into some characteristic shape, as typewriting is said to affect the finger-tips. I asked of my expression if it differed in some subtle manner from the expressions of men who did not fish—who shot, for instance, or collected butterflies. Was it more gentle, or, perhaps, more brutal than theirs? I could find nothing in my hands or my expression that shouted the angler, nor in anything else. There was certainly nothing more clearly piscatorial about my dress-suit than about the dress-suits of other men. Yet within ten minutes of my sitting down to dinner, my partner would say, " I think you fish." After several years, I had rejected all but one of the explanations which had occurred to me. This one follows. In each case before I was presented, my hostess must have addressed the destined woman in some such words as these : "My dear, you have a terrible trial coming to you. But he fishes. Forgive me this once ; it shall never happen again. Remember, he fishes." Simultaneously with this discovery, I abandoned the dining-out habit.

There was, I remember, another thing they always said. They said it immediately after I had replied " Yes " to their observation. It was this: " I always think a fisherman must require so much patience." Then they would continue with : " I'm sure I should never have the patience to fish," or, "How can you find the patience to sit all day with never a bite?" It was then that I would open out and talk to them of angling during the rest of the dinner, which enabled them to listen without inconvenience to all the other conversations of all the other guests. Had they listened to me, they would have learned my reasons for believing that patience is not an essential part of the angler's equipment. But my words might have unsettled their convictions, and no doubt they did well to refuse me their attention, for thoroughly to enjoy one's food one's convictions must be founded on the rock.

This one—about the angler's patience—is so founded. Everyone holds it, except anglers, and anglers—more shame to them!—pretend to, for in their hearts they know that it is false. Yet so unwilling is man to forego an advantage, however acquired, that they do nothing to expose the fallacy of the belief. When the non-angler gives evidence of possessing it, the angler looks smug, even agrees to the monstrous lie, bolsters it up; he has not the common honesty to disclaim the virtue that is attributed to him. This is not as it should be. I propose to demonstrate the impatience of fishermen.

At once the pole-fisher will be adduced. " If

L

patience is not here," it will be said, "where is
it?" See him, immovable, tobacco consuming;
he sits on his camp-stool, permitting his eyes to
creep from side to side as he follows the float
from above him to below him through the long
hours. Here decidedly is patience. I would
premise that I know nothing of pole-fishing; I
speak here of fly-fishing. But in any case the
pole-fisher is no example of patience. The word
implies uncomplaining endurance of evil. The
pole-fisher has no evils to endure. What has he
to complain about? To what wrongs should he
give utterance? He has no wrongs, no great
disasters, no small worries cumulative of effect.
If the fish feed, he has sport; if not, not. In
either case he is ideally placed. He is thoroughly
comfortable. He sits at his ease in his punt.
The water never rushes into his waders. The
trees, the hay, lend greenness to his landscape, not
terror to his casting. The current gives his fore-
arm exercise; does not ruin his cunningest throw.
The wind passes over him, and it is gone; but it
has fanned him, not taken his only serviceable
pattern. The action of the stream removes, from
time to time, the paste or what not from his hook,
thereby giving him something to do. The word
"drag" is not in his vocabulary. Who could not
be 'patient' under such conditions? Yet I have

heard a pole-fisher say appalling things just after losing what he declared to be a specimen bleak.

But, whatever the pole-fisher may be, I say that the fly-fisher is not patient. He is persevering, but he is not patient. The ass is patient under the raining blows of the callous club. Uncomplaining, the ass endures evil. The fly-fisherman is not thus. If evil comes upon him he is not found uncomplaining. Let his flies begin to crack off. The first time it happens he will repair the damage without exhibition of anger; listen to him when the sixth has passed from him down the wind. True, he will persevere in attaching flies until his box, hat, and coat have yielded up the last tattered wing, the last rusty hook; but though he endures, he complains bitterly. But if you would listen to him, you must be concealed. If he knows you are there he will say nothing. Putting a fearful restraint upon himself, he will say nothing, for he values his reputation for patience above his own comfort. Only hide, and you shall hear things.

One of the marked characteristics of the angler is his love of solitude. He is for ever impressing this upon other people. "Company," he will say, "is, in its way, very well; but not when one is fishing. To meet a comrade for lunch at some point on the bank, previously chosen, is delightful. To spend half an hour in idle, pleasant chat makes a welcome break in the business of the day. But when I am actually fishing," he says, "I like to be quite alone." I wonder if it has ever occurred to his non-angling hearers that he may have more reasons than one for his love of solitude? They probably think that he wishes to attune his soul to nature. Not a bit of it! He wants to be able to swear at his ease. Ordinary swearing thrives on companionship; but angling calls for extraordinary swearing, and for this one must be alone. Up to a point swearing is a pleasant and amusing exercise; beyond that point it becomes ridiculous. But to be ridiculous there must be someone to do the ridiculing. An angler in his greater moments of expansion ceases to have any sense of humour, and cannot himself provide the audience necessary to perceive his own ridiculousness. If, then, someone is standing by when one of these great moments comes to him, he is unable to expand, or, if he expands, he becomes ridiculous, and in either case he is uncomfortable. Therefore he declines companionship; therefore he prates about his communion with nature, his love of remote and solitary places, of the broad, empty meadows and the long, silent reaches. Therefore he demands the companionship of the innocent birds and the gentle water-voles. These creatures cannot understand what he is saying. They cannot put him to shame. He can invoke anything or anybody in their hearing without discomfort.

I discovered this great truth some years ago, on this very water, in the following circumstances: I was the sport of a cross wind, a strong current, and five fat fish feeding furiously. When for the sixth or seventh time the familiar crack sounded in my ears, and the gut, lashed with passionate vehemence across the gale, smote the water, and the heavy thud which should have announced the descent of the fly did not happen, then I deliberately and with great labour (I stood up to my middle in the Clere) withdrew my right foot from the soft mud and stamped it violently and without sound back again. This affording me no relief, I addressed flies, fish, wind, water, and myself in one comprehensive and incredibly ridiculous curse. In fancy's full career a movement on shore caused me to turn round, and I perceived our decent miller waddling rapidly away, and shame struck me dumb. Since then I have always insisted on the advantages of complete solitude.

It is easy to reply that I am not a good angler, and have no right to use myself in support of my own proposition. Nay, nay; nothing is said about the patience of good anglers. It is anglers in the mass who are supposed to practise this rare virtue. And, so far as good anglers are concerned, I can only say that, within my experience, the better the angler, the more surely does he value solitude. There may be nothing in this. On the other hand, there may. I think there is.

XXII

OF MR. BLENNERHASSETT FOR THE SECOND TIME

SINCE my first meeting with Mr. Blennerhassett, I have never until to-day happened to find that peremptory gentleman by the riverside. I have not missed him. Such people do not add to the charm of the water-meadows. Living as I do on the very water, I am able to pick and choose my moments for angling, and seldom fish for more than a few hours each day. The Blennerhassett comes from a distance, and cannot always do that. It is scarcely odd, then, that in all this long time I have not encountered him. No, it is only fortunate.

To-day, however, as I sat on a hatch in the lower of the Two Meadows, with my feet in the water, digesting my breakfast and reflecting on the value of the kipper to trout-fishers, I was hailed from behind, and turning perceived Mr. Blennerhassett striding towards me. Next moment he towered above me, and the fish which I had not yet put down abandoned its meal and that part of the Clere.

The Blennerhassett followed its wake with an approving eye. "That's a tidy one," he said. I assented. "I saw him yesterday," he said. "So did I," I replied, wondering if he knew of the two-pounder that feeds under the alder just above that hatch. "Have you," he went on, "such a thing as a light about you? I've left my damned box at home." I handed him my box of safeties. He lit a cigarette, absolutely thanking me. I have seldom been more gratified. "Done anything?" he asked. I said that I never did anything. He informed me that he had only been on the water half an hour, but that he had a fish. I murmured my delight. He opened his basket and exhibited a trout. It was plainly undersized. "This," he said, "is the third damned trout I've had out of this damned river."

Now what is to be said of a man who can damn the Clere? Whatever it is I did not say it. But I observed that he seemed to have had a poor season. Indeed, I knew as much, for Joe has kept me abreast of the doings of my fellow-rods. He said he had. I waited for him still further to qualify his season. I was not disappointed. "A damned poor one," he said. "What fly do you generally use?" he asked. I told him that lately I had found a ginger quill no more inefficacious than other patterns. "I haven't any," he said. "I'd thank you for a couple." I gave him one, but none the less he thanked me as he fastened it to his gut.

"You staying in this field?" he asked. I said I was. It was evident to me that he knew of the two-pounder. "Then," said he, with an anxious glance towards the alder, "I'll be getting on."

I reminded him that he still had my matches.

He took them from his pocket. Then he said: "You live here, don't you?" I said I did. "Well," he said, "it would be very kind of you if you'd let me have these. I'm far from home," he added, with pathetic humour, "and matchless." He was right.

I said: "Please keep the box." He replaced it in his pocket. "Thank you," he said, for the third time. "A cigarette?" He opened a case full of gold-tipped things. Now there is only one cigarette. I declined his magnanimous offer. He looked rather amazed, I thought.

When he had gone quite away I left the meadow and walked about two hundred yards to old Mrs. Pescod's shop, where I got some matches. Then I was able to smoke again.

When 1 got back to the meadow, this Blenner-hassett was kneeling by the hatch flicking my ginger quill towards my two-pound trout.

But he didn't catch it.   It is still there.

XXIII

OF THIS EVENING

THIS night a red sedge and I were in the meadow below Crab Hatch from 9.0 to 10.0, and later. I saw nothing move, caught nothing, cared nothing. The evening was a benediction, dry, warm, still; not a hint of mist anywhere, not a flaw on the mirror of the stream. The sky was a field of cloud picked out in smoky violet with fish scales of darkest brown, but there flared above the valley's elbow one broad band of white light. As I crept along the bank it glinted ghostly among the mysterious fields. And always, dying, it moved steadily into the North. Under the banks lurked endless gloom, and at my feet the thinnest rippling shallow, at this unrevealing hour, seemed motionless, as if the stillness of the night had gripped the very river.

The Valley, by day so bright, so filled with colour and life and feature—the spread carpet of tinted grasses, the swelling golden green walls of turf, the arched canopy of flecked blue, the sombre beech woods, the grey tremulous willows, the brown thatch, the little wreaths of opal smoke, the superb elms that dominate all—the valley was now but a valley of shadows, formless, unguessable. Only the black hedges might be traced against the pallor of field and hill, and the elms, indefinite but unconquered, surged violet-edged over the sky-line. The pollards, too, seemed soft round clouds that had come to rest by the water. On Ottley Down the clump lay like a couched lion, rather terrible of aspect. It was as if some great beast of the night had come early to the hill's edge, and now waited for utter darkness before it descended upon the village.

On the rail of the wooden bridge I leaned and stared after the sun, and thanked God that 1 am not as other men are, such men as, at that same moment, might be clearing their way remorselessly, with a fair thing upon their arm, towards a buffet. On the bridge one had no company but oneself. One had elbow-room, at any rate. Had a certain fair thing been with me, I had been well content, but she was gone to bed like a sensible woman.

And I listened to the sounds of the night.

There are more of these by the stream than elsewhere, on the road, or in the fields. There stealthy, dry little noises come out of the hedges where the field people go about their business. A goat-sucker may purr, a horse snort, a cow low, a cock give tongue. But these may all be heard by the river, and the river adds to them a number of sounds all its own. Against the piles of the bridge the water runs with a barely perceptible chuckle. A coot clucks far off. A water-rat, coasting in the blackness, plunges as one moves. The big trout flop over after the fat sedge flies. And now and then loud sucking sounds break out under the banks. I have been taught to believe the frogs to be responsible for these vulgar noises.

All is peace.

But to-night, somewhere up stream, there was a heavy, lunging splash, followed by a thin pitiful squeaking; then silence. Another heavier splash, three faint feeble cries, and again silence.

And again silence. It was over, whatever it was. The incident was closed. But the night did not seem so sweet as heretofore, and I came indoors.

XXIV

OF THE PERFECT THRILL

I ONCE read in a book on fishing these words: "No angler who has not landed a trout upon a fly of his own making can say that he has known the perfect thrill." Now, I am an amateur of thrills and sensations of every kind. I believe that every thrill, whether it be gained in the concert-room, in the theatre, at the dinner-table, or in pursuit of sport, is worth knowing, and to get a new one I will take any trouble. As far as the thrills of trout-fishing go, I had thought, before I read the words which I have quoted, that they were exhausted, always excepting the never-to-be-exhausted thrill of landing the largest-fish-yet. I had caught trout in all sorts of places, though, perhaps, not with all sorts of lures. I had never, for example, employed either poison or dynamite, but there are sensations which an angler, however curious and refined his taste may be, must deny himself.

And here was a thrill which I did not know. This alone made it attractive. But the "perfect"

thrill ! Gods ! Was there any resisting such
a promise ? And so simply won ! The condition
precedent to this unimagined and supreme experience was the mere tying of a fly. At that
time I knew that fly-tying was the easiest thing
in the world. It wanted a knack. But what was
a knack that it should stand in the way of my
realising the perfect thrill ? Anyone can acquire
a knack. A little effort, a little patience, a few
failures, and lo ! one day the knack comes, and
you wonder why you could not do it from the
first.

This vision of the perfect thrill was given to me
on an early day of a rather recent April. I think,
to be as accurate as possible, that it was the first
of the month. My whole soul consumed with
eagerness, I cabbed it to a tackle-shop and bought
a small handbook on fly-tying. I read this book
in an hour. I had not been mistaken. Fly-tying
was the easiest thing in the world. I cabbed it
back to the tackle-shop and bought a vice, some
dozens of assorted eyed hooks, many reels of
brightly coloured silk, two pairs of delicately
curved scissors, half a dozen forceps, a pound
of beeswax, a bottle of liquid wax, a quantity
of dubbin, some rare furs, and an "indispensable"
packet of hackle and wing-feathers. I got, as an
afterthought, a few pike scales and a jeweller's

eyeglass. On my way home from my office, I stopped at Leadenhall Market and bought a fowl with all its feathers on. These purchases cost me a great deal of money, but who cares for money where the perfect thrill is in question ?

Next morning I was still ungifted with any knack that could be called a knack. The silk broke very vexingly, I found, and the liquid wax was rather ubiquitous, and the hackles did not seem to wind on to the hooks quite so easily as the little treatise said they did ; but these were early days to look for great results. During the following Sunday afternoon I called on a friend who boasted himself a tier of flies. In the course of our conversation I mentioned that I had never seen him make a fly, and suggested that he should do so now. He agreed in the most amiable way, sat down there and then at his bench, took a few things out of a cigar-box, and evolved a pale olive in the twinkling of an eye. I said, "Oh, *that's* how you do it ! " He had, as far as I could see, done none of the things which the book laid down as essential. He replied that some did it one way and others another way. That was how *he* did it. It was, he added, only a little knack that one had to get. He made several other flies for me, and wanted me to try my hand, but I said No, I had no ambition of that kind. I went

away, resolved to invite him to my home one day
soon and paralyse him with my unsuspected skill.

Two months passed, and I had not known the
perfect thrill. But although my duns had been
rejected, hope did not die, for the May-fly was
coming on. Making a dun is admittedly a nig-
gling job. But a May-fly is a large, robust
creature, and its imitation may be attempted with
some confidence. It is a thing one can lay hold
of and pull about with one's hands. Finesse (or
so I thought) is not of the essence of May-fly
making. I made a May-fly and went down into
Wiltshire, the premonition of the perfect thrill
already tingling at my nerve centres. I cast my
line towards a magnificent trout and waited for
the result. The trout, giving one glance of terror
upwards, fled for its life into a thick bunch of
weeds, while the surface of the river Clere was
broken in every direction by the torpedo rushes
of great fish which were copying his discreet
example.

I now lost a good deal of my interest in fly-
tying. I made up my mind to master it in the
winter, when time cannot be wasted. A little
later I went to that island in the Arctic Circle
where MacAlister and I found out the inner truth
of flounder-fishing. Here such fish as the poachers
had left to us were innocent of guile. I caught

M

my first of these trout on a large red Pennell,
and, having thus discovered the only fly that was
the slightest use, I stuck to it until my small
provision was threatened with exhaustion. This
disturbed me considerably, for I knew that none
of the other two gross of patterns which I had
bought before I left London were any good at all,
and my thoughts turned naturally to my new art
and my box of fly-tying apparatus. The second
of these I found had been left in England. The
first, however, was at my finger-tips, and my
materials were not difficult to get. Your true
fisherman can always find an expedient. I made
a red Pennell out of the hook of another fly, a
ryper, and some red worsted which I took from a
deep-sea spoon-bait which happened to be in my
fly-box. I found, too, some gay tinsel on a lamp-
shade in the drawing-room of my hostess. As my
copy differed slightly from the original I named it
The Unapproachable. Then I stepped calmly to
the edge of a bottomless lake and began to fish.
At the forty-second cast a 4-oz. char of incredible
bravery seized my masterpiece and attempted to
drag it into the depths. A gentle touch of the
wrist, and all was over. The char was in a bush
of bog-myrtle behind my back. I had caught a
fish upon a fly of my own making.

The perfect thrill? Well, I confess I was disappointed in a perfect thrill. But that may be because my fish was not a trout. But, trout or char, I feel that it might have been keener after all my labour in searching for it. I shall never feel it, whatever it is, for I buy my flies now. But then I am, and always shall be, a very low-class angler.

XXV

OF A WAR WITH BRAN-NEWCOME

HERE follows the story of Bran-Newcome, with whom, in a certain year of rain and wind, I had to do. Read and you shall learn of our little private war, how it began in the early days of May, and how articles of peace were signed on the twenty-eighth of June under the willows on the bank that lies between the Running Ditch and the Slow Water by the road to Great Ottley.

This was in the good old days when I used to catch fishes out of Clere, the bad old days when the angling had no competition, and I used to come rushing down here by a leaden-footed express train each Friday night and go away on Monday morning and fish perpetually in between, the bad old days when there was no harp in the valley—only the fishes and me.

You are to know that the Slow Water is not all mine to fish. From half-way along it down to the island the main stream is forbidden to me. At the top of this alien territory is a strong fence some eight feet high, which projects not less than three feet into the stream. Along its top an incalculable number of sharp hooks have been driven. Among these hooks and around this wood, wherever possible, barbed wire has been wound with a lavish hand. No expense has been spared to make this fence impregnable. A notice-board, moreover, threatens with penalties those who shall violate the rights of piscary of Sir Abinger Bran-Newcome. But no mere process of law could have any terrors for the resolute soul which could even contemplate an assault upon a position of such obvious strength. I have never seen a fishing boundary which it was more impossible to ignore. Such a fortification is an insult. The man who raises it and maintains it shows that he classes his neighbours with the housebreaker and the horse-thief and the burner of ricks. To catch his fishes—if lawfully it may be done—becomes a meritorious act.

When, therefore, I reached this spot on my first visit for that long-ago year and saw a trout rise under the far bank just opposite the fence, I did not inquire too closely into his precise position in relation to the boundary, but cast over him eagerly and put him down without much trouble. From subsequent observation, I am able to state that a line drawn at right angles to the course of the stream from the point of the fence to the opposite bank would have passed through that trout, just behind the gills. So my mind is quite easy. His head was in my water. Let the other fellow have his tail. Having put this trout down, I passed on; and so much for our preliminary skirmish.

I thought no more about him till the next day when, approaching the place, I remembered the rise of the day before and came warily to the bank. A short description of the theatre of war may not be superfluous.

I was confined here to one side of the river, which at this point is about twenty yards broad. No one can wade in the Slow Water and live. The bank is three feet high. A line of tall willows fringes it thickly. One of them is missing, the one next the fence. This alone makes it possible to cast across the stream. Crouching close to the fence and working the point perpendicularly, it can be done, for I learned to do it. On one's immediate right the entanglements of Sir Bran menace rod and tackle. On one's immediate left is a spreading willow. Oh, it was a happy little corner for a bungling fool to fish away in it some of the best hours of his life.

The position, then, demands a perfectly straight

cut across the water. Now on every day on which I fished during that May and most of that June, the river was very high and the wind was from the right, strong and down stream. So, unless the line was thrown very loosely on to the water the heavy current caught it instantly, the fly was dragged out into the middle with a wake like a motor-boat and the fish was put down.

The position from my point of view was deplorable. For who was I—who am I, just Heaven!—to spare line when I am throwing to a fish twenty yards away?

Nevertheless, stimulated by the sight of the fence, I waded through the Running Ditch and wallowed through the wet grass, as yet not very high (though very wet), till I was able to look at the water. My fish was hard at work. Nothing that came his way went past him. I could see him plainly—a good trout about 2 lb. weight lying just under the bank in a little bay. I made my dispositions—my ridiculous, presumptuous dispositions. I tied on some silly fly or other—unless I had one on already, which vital point in my narrative I confess I forget. I got out my absurd line; I made my asinine allowance for the wind, and I cast. When the wind and the current had done their worst with my lure, the fish had gone away.

Now, because in those days I still had some troublesome ideas about those things which it is proper for a dry-fly angler to do, I waited there among the great man-eating nettles for ten long minutes, and was just about to release myself when the trout came back and began to gulp duns as if he was mad. On that occasion I put him down four times.

It was on the Sabbath that I named him Bran-Newcome. On this day I drove him off almost at once because my fly, at the first delicate cast, became involved among the hooks and wire of my neighbour's landmark, and I had to stand up and make an exhibition of myself. I went back to London next day, but I was burdened with a great oath to bring Bran-Newcome to grass before the season should be out. One undertakes these obligations lightly, not realising what they mean. Had I been in my senses I should have agreed with myself to consider Bran-Newcome a small, ill-conditioned trout, or I should have remembered that my title to fish for him was dubious. I should have left him to my neighbour behind his rampart. But in truth I was possessed by the fish.

All through May, whenever I was in Willows, I was always going up to that fence to see if he was feeding. My sport higher up and lower down

stream was ruined by the thought that he might
be feeding. I could not enjoy my own food because he might be enjoying his. I saw him at it
as 1 fell asleep at night. I woke muttering his
name. He got between me and my work in
London, though I did not mind this at all. The
moment I reached Willows I was off to the fence.
I was no better than a purist.

I skip five woeful weeks.

I would have you suppose the nettles growing
higher and fiercer, the burdocks waxing ranker,
the hemlocks stronger through which I wormed
my way daily, amongst which I swore and swel-
tered, as I laid for the life of Bran-Newcome;
the meadow-sweet growing more luxuriant, the
willow-branches more spreading, the barbed wire
ever more tough in which I caught and lost my
flies. But on the twenty-eighth of June—ah! on
the twenty-eighth of June—I caught him.

Who cares about the pattern of fly, or the state
of the weather? Who cares how he fought? These
are petty matters. Believe me, 1 caught him.
I say, I caught him. He lay at my feet. The
day was mine. He would flout me no more. I
could angle for other fishes.

I took up the landing-net.

And then—I knew that I could not kill him.
I had come to endow this fish with a personality,

to regard him as an enemy to my peace of mind,
to picture him to myself as an incarnation of all
the vices, to feel that to rid the river of his accursed
presence was a sacred duty—I had conceived a
positive hatred of him. Yet, as I poised the net
handle above his skull I caught his eye, and it
unmanned me as the eye of C. Marius unmanned
the Gaul whom they sent to dispatch him. Bran-
Newcome's eye was an honest eye, the eye of a
decent, peaceable, hardworking stay-at-home. In
it I read none of that extreme malevolence towards
myself with which I had credited him. There
was not even resentment in it. It was only the
silly frightened eye of a fish out of water. He
did not know who or what I was. Did he so
much as connect me with his present inability
to breathe? My estimate of Bran-Newcome's
character changed as suddenly as it had been
formed gradually. No; our relations had grown
too personal, too intimate. I was taken with a
kind of shame to think that I could meditate the
assassination of this companion of so many good
hours by the water. Even as the Gaul threw
away his sword, so I threw away my net, and I
cried aloud: "I cannot slay Bran-Newcome!"
I laid him in the stream; he swam slowly away;
and I have never seen him again.

I used to do silly things like that—in those

days, when I used to catch many fishes out of the Clere.

Can it be that Generosity is the Child of Affluence? Can it? Can it?

XXVI

OF SPECIALISED CONVERSATION AND
OF A DINNER

CHAVENDER has been here again, drinking tea and killing my fishes. With him came Wickham.

My wife and I are lovers of good talk, and these two men are notable talkers. We had both promised ourselves much pleasure from their whimsicalities, and had consoled ourselves for the loss of their society, during the first day of their visit, by the anticipation of that which they would say to us, and to one another, when they should finally be driven within doors by the darkness. This first day, then, drew at length to a close, and after the waders of Wickham and Chavender had been removed, after Chavender's first cup of tea had been poured out—that is to say, about quarter-past ten at night—we were, the four of us, seated in the drawing-room, and I told the company about the angling which I had done that day. Now, I had not fished above two evening hours altogether, for I had wished my guests to have their will of the water, and my wife and I had spent the afternoon with the ass on the downs. Still, I had a tale to tell, though a tale of failure and disappointment, and I told it. This occupied our attention till shortly before eleven, when Wickham practically insisted on a hearing.

This had been Wickham's first experience of the Clere, and he had a great deal to say. During the day he had been over the whole water. So, beginning at the Lower End, he told us about several fishes which he had seen there. These were all well known to Chavender and to me, but it was not always that we could be perfectly satisfied as to the identity of any particular one about which Wickham was talking. For Wickham had not that perfect knowledge of the water which Chavender, after an acquaintance of three days, and I, after an intimacy of five and a half seasons, possess. Still, with a little care, we were always able to discover which of the trouts was the subject of Wickham's remarks, and to follow his proceedings with almost as much pleasure and knowledge as if we had actually assisted at them. Our talk ran something like this.

WICK : So *he* was put down for good. Then I went on, and just round the next corner I saw a sneaking rise in a quiet place, beside some rushes.

I : I know the beast. On the far side he lies, just below a drain.

CHAVEN : No, that one's in the next meadow. Wickham means the one about sixty yards above the third plank.

I : There's no corner for a good hundred yards above the third plank.

CHAVEN : That depends on what you call a corner. There's a distinct bend——

WICK : This was a corner. Turns to the left.

I : To the right, you mean.

CHAVEN : Oh ! *that's* the one you mean. *That* one's right up beyond the hedge. *That's* the one under the alder.

WICK : No. There wasn't any alder. The bank's quite clear.

I : Well, which side *was* he ?

WICK : My side.

I : *Your* side ? Nonsense !

CHAVEN : Of course. He's about a pound and a half.

I : You don't mean the one with the white mark ?

CHAVEN : No, that's about twenty yards above Wickham's fish.

WICK : No. I saw *him* just before I got to the one I'm telling you about. About thirty yards below. But he saw me and bolted. Besides, this one round the corner was a good pound and three-quarters.

CHAVEN: Oh, I know. There's a twig sticks up just outside him, a black twig.

WICK: Well, blackish.

CHAVEN: There's a young copper beech opposite.

WICK: Yes, youngish.

I: Oh, *that* one.

WICK: Yes.

CHAVEN: Of course.

WICK: Well——

At this point my wife suddenly began to favour us with some very pungent observations. She said, among other things, that she had not asked Wickham and Chavender to Willows that they might entertain her with this kind of prating. She asked them plainly if they had left their wits behind them in London. She expressed astonishment that two such splendid intellects could concern themselves with folly of so colossal an order. She threatened to remove the teapot if Chavender so much as said "trout" again. For a week, she said, she had been living for that witty discourse upon really interesting topics of which she knew them to be capable. She called Heaven to witness, that of all tedious subjects angling was the most tiresome. Them and their copper beeches! Them and their measurements along the bank! Them and their planks and their fishes with white marks and their dirty little twigs!

I tried in vain to point out that the twig in question, being laved perpetually by the crystal water of the fairest stream on earth, could not be otherwise than spotless, but she would not hear a word in defence of Chavender and Wickham. She poured pitiless scorn upon their innocent fishing talk—the poor fellows. Nay, she parodied it, exhibiting a knowledge of its character and a keen appreciation of its possibilities in this direction with which I could never have credited her. It seems out of all reason that a woman who, up to a few short weeks ago, had never so much as seen a chalk-stream, should have gained such an insight into the manner in which dry-fly anglers communicate with one another.

True, I have seldom come in to a meal during all our time here without giving her some little account of my morning's sport, And whenever I have had a fish to show, I have generally described its situation, the state of the wind, the brightness or dullness of the weather, and perhaps drawn a diagram of the place showing the force and direction of the currents or the disposition of natural obstacles to success. And I am not surprised that she should be familiar with the names and appearances of many of the commoner artificial

patterns. But I confess that she surprised me.
Here is one more evidence of her quick apprehension. And I bear witness that she amused me.
It was indescribably ludicrous to hear her travesty
of Wickham's description of his first fish and how
he grassed it. I am sure Chavender blessed himself that he had not yet launched forth. This, of
course, put an end to all angling talk, and thereafter we discussed the Drama and other really
vital things.

I am sorry that Chavender and Wickham
talked shop, because though I, personally, was
able to enjoy all that they might have said about
fishing, my wife was not, and it is not proper that
she should be teased with stuff which does not
interest her. Fishermen sometimes forget that all
the world is not agog to hear of their exploits.
Yet fishermen are not the only offenders.

This power to bore with special conversation is
a product of this specialised age. There was,
there must have been, a time when, everybody
knowing everything that was known, it was impossible for two or more to discuss any matter
which was outside the knowledge of a third, fourth,
or fifth as the case might be. The cave-parties of
the first men can never have suffered from " shop."
To-day, however, as it is impossible for anybody
to be omniscient, as it becomes more and more

N

necessary for everybody to specialise in their oc-
cupations, so special amusements become more
and more the rule. No longer does a gentleman
excel at hunting and hawking, archery, swordsman-
ship, the lute, the improvisation of verses, and a
dozen other accomplishments. To-day he has
time only for golf, or cricket, or lawn-tennis,
or what not. Even in the field of sport competition is too keen to allow of excellence in
more than one branch, save in the case of a few
astonishing persons, whose renown is the best
evidence of this condition of affairs.

Therefore it is very easy to-day for two people
to talk with pernicious effect upon a third ; and as
conversation, if it is pleasant, tends to follow what
some people, among them myself, call "the line
of least resistance," this disaster is a common
one.

I have often speculated as to which is the worst
shop. For a long time I thought it was the
golfer's variety, but my opinion was altered by a
discussion based on the performances of league
teams. Hunting shop is very generally hated,
though I suspect this hatred to be the result of
jealousy. Chess shop is dreary enough, but no
worse to a person who does not understand that
so-called game than, say, musical shop to one who
knows nothing of classical music. And the shop

of Knurr and Spell has no superiority to others which I have heard.

I fancy that all kinds prove equally exasperating to those who cannot join the talk, equally delightful to those who can.

But there is one kind of special conversation which, I submit, has a peculiarly atrocious flavour for the uninstructed, than which I can imagine no mere game shop that can more deplorably affect the enforced listener. For as no kind of talk is more absorbing to the majority of people than the discussion, the praise, the censure of their common acquaintances, so no kind can be more odious when the persons discussed are unknown to the victim of this shop. For to the ordinary annoyances of other people's special conversation is added the keen desire to join in, with which no other kind afflicts the listener. Nobody wants to enter a discussion of stamp collectors if he be not himself a philatelist. He is bored, and there is an end of it. But if these stamp collectors turn from their water-marks and their errors to the idiosyncrasies of some unknown James, then does the bored become the frantic, for he thinks, "Did I but know this James, with what point and venom could I criticise him! How humorously I could take him off! With what lively exaggerations could

I embroider the anecdotes that I should relate
of him!"

I will tell you a little story.

On one of the most unfortunate nights of my
life I reached a certain hotel, believing that I was
to entertain to dinner a man who had just
descended there. From this festivity I anticipated
a great deal of pleasure. The invitation was five
years old. For five years I had been hungering
for this dinner, at which my dear old Derry and I
were going to celebrate his return from the East.
He was in this hotel. He had sent me a telegram
to say that he was my man for the evening. All
the way to the hotel I had cogitated worthy
menus.

As I entered the lounge I perceived Derry,
and precipitated myself across the intervening
space. After we had greeted each other, I found
that he was introducing me to Mr. Thoms, just
home from the Straits, one of the best, etcetera,
etcetera. Mr. Thoms had all the appearance of
being that moment landed in England after a
protracted sojourn in Asia; that is to say, his
clothes were obviously those in which six or seven
years earlier, a slim boy, he had fared forth into the
mysterious East. And the East had fattened
him. To-morrow he would be at his tailor's, and
the day after to-morrow he would be undistinguish-

able from anybody else.   At this moment, however, he had a very unusual kind of appearance.

"The dinner," said Derry, "is on me.   Thoms dines with us."

I did not want to dine with Thoms, but I could not say so ; not, at least, while I was in the very act of shaking Thoms by the hand.   I wished to dine with Derry on food carefully chosen by myself, and sit far into the night discoursing with Derry of our past lives, where they had touched, and of the people that we knew.   The presence of Thoms must make all this impossible.   It must impose a strictly impersonal tone upon our conversation.   Well, I can enjoy impersonal talk as much as anyone.   Thoms had an intelligent face.   And the poor devil was alone, save for us, on this his first night in London, after an age of exile.   Resolved to get Derry to myself at an early date, I accepted the situation.

We passed to a gilded, blatant place where they serve a *table d'hôte* dinner and have a band.   Such was Derry's choice.   As he named it to the cab-man I thought of the peaceful, silent isolation-ward in which my club dines its guests, and I sighed.

In the cab Derry and Thoms continued the conversation which I had interrupted.   They continued it further in the restaurant.

It was about British people then resident in the East, or home on leave, or voyaging between England and ultimate Asia. It was about nothing else. The names of these people were in many cases the names of people that I knew, but I could never discover that Derry and Thoms were acquainted with any of these friends of mine.

There were, for instance, two men called Hay about whom they talked for nearly the whole of one course. When they began, I had a fleeting hope that one of them might be Hay the stockbroker, a man I would gladly have criticised adversely. But it was only Hay of Penang. And their other Hay was Hay of Perak, cousin of the first Hay, and quite unconnected with the Stock Exchange. It was either Corbould or "Bruggy" Cotton that Thoms had passed at Singapore or Suez on his way back from England to Johore or the Chagos Archipelago. In either case the dear old chap was looking as fit as a flea after his leave. Barnes had gone to Christmas Island. Anson had married money. There had been the devil to pay at Labuan, but probably Derry had heard about that. No, Derry had heard nothing. Here Thoms became aware of my presence, which he had forgotten, and his discretion caused him to speak about the appointment of old Billy K. to Selangore. No doubt at some future time Derry would be enlightened concerning the Labuan trouble. Thoms understood that Maitland and his wife were on their way home, but he feared that he would miss Saunders, who was due back at Sandakan in a month. T. A. was a daddy at last. Good old T. A. We drank the health of T. A. and of Mrs. T. A. and of their offspring, but I never had more particular information about them, and I cannot tell you the sex of the child, because Derry wanted to know where Giles was now, and Thoms thought that he was still in Daru. But I remember that somebody else had been shifted to quite another place, the name of which I forget. It was, however, close to another place where death had recently robbed Derry and Thoms of a dear old boy they had known. Poor old chap! I wonder if he had been worrying too much over the Labuan trouble.

Our dinner at last came to an end. I had known from the first that, Thoms being just off his steamboat, the Empire could by no means be avoided. Nor was it. In the stalls Derry and Thoms continued cheerfully to converse about unknown people, by their initials and nicknames. I do not think they had any understanding of that which was happening on the stage. They never looked that way; they never looked my way, either. Yet I was close beside them. They amazed me.

They still amaze me. I can even now hardly believe that these things really took place.

Now, I still tried to love Derry. The memory of what he had been was not yet totally effaced. Besides, I had promised him a dinner five years ago, and as a man of honour I must carry out my engagement. Therefore, near the end of the performance, I asked him if he would dine with me at my club on the following evening, for I knew that he was to be but two nights in London on this occasion. He answered that he had already promised to dine that night with Thoms. There followed a constrained silence, which Thoms at length broke by saying that he hoped I would dine with him and Derry. To this I replied that I had an engagement for to-morrow night to dine with some old friends out of which I could not possibly escape. Then there was another constrained silence.

I have never seen either Derry or Thoms again.

That is why I am able so heartily to sympathise with my wife when she found the fishing talk of Wickham and Chavender insupportable. That is why I insisted upon their talking about the drama.

XXVII

OF A FALSE BALANCE

AND while I am concerned with Chavender
and Wickham, let me tell you a thing. On
their last night I brought in a trout. I declared
it at one pound and three-quarters; this on the
authority of my weighing machine. Chavender
said, "Nonsense." I swore it. I produced my
weighing machine. I hung the trout on it. The
thing dipped to one and three-quarters. "Amazing!" said Chavender. I was nettled. There is
nothing amazing in my taking a trout of a pound
and three-quarters. I have had several this season
already. "I suppose," I sneered, "you would only
allow it a pound and a half." But I had done this
sterling fellow an injustice. He shook his head.
"I could have sworn," he said, "that this fish is
over two pounds." He weighed it in his hand.
Then he produced his own weighing machine and
hung the trout. Then he pointed to the needle,
which pointed to two pounds and a quarter.
"Your balance," said he, "weighs short by
half a pound. The spring is far too strong."

There is something superhuman about such conduct.

Now, it is impossible and would be ungrateful to doubt the correctness of the weighing machine used by a fisherman so notable as is Chavender. It would also be idiotic. I have accepted his verdict upon my balance without a murmur.

So I have been catching great fishes all summer. I have been returning to their stream trouts a pound and a half heavy as beneath my consideration, and only the greatest anglers do this. My rare two-pounders have been two-and-a-half-pounders, and as all two-and-a-half-pounders really weigh three, three pounds has been the actual weight of these fishes. Yes, I have been enjoying my sport far more than I have done. I am vastly beholden to Chavender. And I find that I must revise the sport of a lifetime. Mine is an old weighing machine, and surely it is reasonable to suppose that the older a spring is the slacker it gets. Now all my fishes have been weighed on this spring. Who knows how grossly it was out five or six years ago. I daresay as much as a pound or a pound and a half. This proves some of the fishes which I caught in those days to have been colossal. Hitherto I have boasted of nothing heavier than three pounds. I can safely call that greatest trout a four-and-a-half-pounder. If not five.

In a few more years my weighing machine will be old enough to make it six.

And may I not safely conclude that the incorrectness of this too powerful spring varies with the weight of the fishes. If a pound fish, for instance, is really one of a pound and a half, I expect a half-pound fish is no more than three-quarters of a pound. But a two-pounder is really three, a three-pounder four and a half, and a five-pounder seven.

This is obviously the only safe way to reckon.

A bright future opens before me.

XXVIII

OF A GORSEDD AT THE GREAT STONES

YESTERDAY I was a wholly undistinguished person. To-day I am a Bard. The manner of it was as follows :—

About midday a number of Welsh, to some of whom we are related by the closest ties of blood and affection, arrived from London in a char-à-banc at our garden gate, and with loud barbaric cries summoned us forth. We were indeed prepared for their coming, and believed that an ordinary picnic was intended. A drive of a few miles, an open-air feast within the Great Stones which illustrate this neighbourhood, a drive back to Willows, tea and farewell—this was the programme which in our simplicity we had imagined. We had yet to learn how the Celt makes holiday.

Nothing excessively unusual happened until luncheon had been eaten. It is true that our companions sang hilariously in Welsh all the way up the Valley, and it is a fact that they gathered great sprays of young oak and fastened them in their hats. But these things, in comparison with that which followed, were the mere commonplaces of ordinary life. We were no more out of the way in Clere valley than, say, a circus. But as I was mopping up sugar with my last strawberry (and I sat just outside the Stones), I perceived that the mother of the two children who were with us was draping her progeny in ample veils of gauze—the lad in green, the girl in white, and close beside them stood a tall and lovely lady who wrapped blue muslin about her head and shoulders. And it was suddenly borne in upon my understanding that I was to be the witness of amazing occurrences. Hardly had I arrived at this conclusion when a respected member of His Majesty's Government sprang upon a recumbent stone and emitted several piercing cries which, I have since been told, gave those present (or such of them as understood him) to know that the Gorsedd was opened.

Now a Gorsedd is a competition for Bardic honours.

At this there arose, swathed in green muslin and crowned with oak, the Druid Derwen, aged ten, who stood stoutly on a Stone and gave forth a Welsh Ode, composed by himself in honour of the Great Circle. And we all stood by and shouted "Clywch! Clywch!" in the manner of the

Welsh when they applaud noble sentiments combined with skilful versification. And while this
was happening a body of two hundred young
women, all wearing straw hats with red ribbons,
arrived in several chars-à-bancs at the Stones, and
coming into the circle stood at first astounded,
and thereafter very properly formed audience for
the children's play, and were silent while the Gorsedd proceeded. And after the Druid Derwen,
the Druidess Caerwys, aged twelve—and she stood
on yet another Stone—in turn gave forth her Ode,
also addressed to the Stones, and we cried "Clywch!
Clywch!" as became those who listened to valiant
poetry. And during this ode certain soldiers with
red crosses on their arms added themselves to our
number, and the policeman came, he who guards
the place from Americans who want to take it
away, and two or three cyclists. And they were
all amazed at the utterances of the Druidess
Caerwys, and looked from the one to the other as
much as to say, "What the devil is all this here?"
But no notice was taken of them because we were
engaged on a very serious business, and they were
gross Lloegrwys, and unworthy to comprehend
these mysteries.

So the Druidess Caerwys ceased and stood down,
and all these chance witnesses of our Bardic doings
imagined that the game of the odd children was

over. But lo ! there leaped upon a fourth Stone a learned counsel and member of Parliament, aged— well, middle-aged, who proceeded to deliver him- self of a flood of ancient British, and he was Llew Towy, the Crownéd Bard of this Gorsedd. And to him replied that reverend Minister of His Majesty (who was in truth none other than the Arch Druid Callestr) and together they had it, antiphonally, and what they said I do not know, but I marked a closing together of the straw-hatted females, and the ambulance men were obviously preparing for work, and the policeman began to look professional, and the cyclists seemed glad that they had their swift machines handy.

And every time that the little knot of supporters cried, " Clywch ! Clywch ! " the eyes of all those persons turned apprehensively in our direction.

Then came the granting of Bardic Honours. Each of us, in turn, arm in arm between Nansi Hir, the lady in blue muslin, and the Druidess Caerwys, was led before the Arch Druid. Then the Crownéd Bard said precisely what he pleased about us—it sounded very abusive, but I am assured that it was all compliments—in support of our pretensions, and the Arch Druid, laying hands upon us, called us by our Bardic names, cracked a jest at our expense, as we knelt before him, and let us go.

And my wife's Bardic name is Telynores yr Amerig, because of the harp and her origin. And my Bardic name is Pen Twadl, which is no doubt one of the compliments.

All this accompanied by " Clywch ! Clywch !" and incessant laughter from those who assisted. But the chief actors might have been at a funeral.

Then we closed this Gorsedd of the Great Stones with a song called " Hen wlad fy Nhadau," and climbing instantly into our char-à-banc, sped back to Willows speaking with tongues and enormously elated.

This is true.

XXIX

OF AN OLD-TIME ANGLER

THE afterglow lingered long in the sky, for it was Midsummer Day and settled weather The West was a sea of pale primrose, where a few long purple cloud-islands floated. It was as if one stood on a height above some fairy Benbecula, flat, dove-coloured, and marked its coast-line in innumerable inlets (where celestial sea-trout ran) reach out for ever to a horizon that was not. Behind me a peerless spire soared from amidst the dark green of elms, as if it would lose itself in the rose of the upper air. I stood on ancient turf, which had laid its seemly carpet of green velvet between odorous flower beds and tall, trim hedges, straight to the old house, where shone a single red window. Ten inches below my feet flowed the river, primrose out of that primrose sea, broad, silent, swift, to mingle almost instantly with woods, where night already dwelt. Large, oily rings appeared here and there upon the surface of the water, spread, died away, were succeeded by others, larger, oilier. The stillness was broken only by the sound of great fish feeding rapidly, greedily, on sedge flies. I cast and cast. The frenzy was upon me that is born of the last moment of daylight, a rise of the big ones, and—an empty creel.

Over the turf, silently, there came towards me a dim figure, which as it approached resolved itself into the likeness of a lively old man, clothed in black, with an apron and gaiters upon his shapely legs, and a low-crowned, broad hat upon his head. His round cheeks were apples, his nose was coloured by nothing but the soundest port, yet his eyes were bright and youthful—a rotund, comfortable elder. Lace ruffles were at his wrists, and a pair of bands depended below his two ample chins. I assumed him to be some dignitary of the cathedral with an old-fashioned taste in dress. A huge creel was slung over his plump shoulders, and in his hand he bore a tremendous fishing-rod. These things placed him among the fraternity.

He said, " Master, well met ! " and I understood him to be a facetious old gentleman. Humour was out of harmony with my mood, but I strove to be civil. " Grammercy ! " said I, " vastly well met ! " He did not smile, and I put him down as one of those humorists whom their own wit alone entertains, and went on fishing. Minutes were precious. I was aware that he remained beside me. Presently: "So ends another merry Mid-summer Day," he observed, and I heard a faint sigh follow the words. "It has brought me right good sport whose memory shall sweeten all my long year." Evidently he got a day on the water each season. I tried to be glad that he had done well—I said I was; but my voice was not convincing. He detected its false ring instantly. "And you, good master," he said, "have catched, I doubt not, an honest store of fishes?" I said, not too amiably (or too truthfully—but who can blame me?) that I had risen several big trout, but had grassed nothing all day. This latter statement the condition of my creel made necessary. He was just the sort of complacent old creature who would not be satisfied with verbal evidence. "Tush, tush!" he observed, "what make of angler is this?" I considered whether I might, without all loss of self-respect, take this venomous ancient by his admirable middle and heave him into the river. I decided that at all costs I must keep my hands off him. I owed my fishing to a churchman, and the clergy hang together.

I busied myself with casting above some particularly oily rings. "And yet," he remarked critically to the sunset, "he throweth deftly and far. But why kneeleth he?"

I rose abruptly and went fifty yards up stream.

I have seldom done a ruder thing, but I was not myself. And this was nothing to what I could have done had I not been resolved to show him forbearance. I stared miserably at water which nothing broke. The first spectral wreaths of the river mists were lightening the darkness upon the further bank.

"Good master,"—unheard he had rejoined me— "prithee suffer a brother angler to make closer acquaintance with that so-far-throwing wand." I held out my split cane to him dumbly. He did not take it, but he bent over it, peering at it through the small square spectacles he wore. "Aye," he said, " a pretty tool and a valiant. But what device is this?" "That," said I, in scorn of him, " is the reel. You perceive, simple sir, that the line, passing through these excellently contrived rings upon the so-valiant wand is retained upon a central drum, and may be drawn off" (I drew some off) " or rolled up at will by the miraculous turning of this deft little pin." I wound up, as ironically as I might.

Again my humour failed to touch him. His eyes were round with amazement and delight. " Is it even so ?" he breathed reverently. I perceived that I had to do with a lunatic or a supreme artist, in either of which cases everything must be forgiven him. Humouring him or playing up to him—I

cared not which, for the rise was over—I indicated
the gut trace. "This," I said, "is the gut, made
by extending the entrails of the silkworm. See
how strong it is, and how transparent." I tugged
at it. "And see here is the fly—a sedge. There
are five hundred other patterns (sold at half a crown
a dozen), all of which I have in these boxes." I
opened my creel, and permitted him to peep
within. "This," I went on, "is my bottle of
paraffin oil, with which I anoint the fly to make it
float more yarely, and so deceive and master these
subtle fishes. These are the pincers with which I
pick my flies out of their boxes. Here is a tube of
dubbin—I smear it on my line, reverend bloke, and
this causes it to float most excellently. Thus with
but one little twitch I do hook the brutes. Here
is a piece of blotting-paper to dry my flies withal if
haply they be wetted. Here——"

"Good gentleman," he said, interrupting, "no
more, I pray you! I am dazed. Tell me but
one thing. How cometh it that with so many
cunning aids thy skill, which sufficeth surely, as I
have seen, hath brought nothing to land in a long
day's angling?" I was silent. A question at once
more pertinent and more impertinent had never
yet been put to me, or one less easy to answer.
"Behold," he said, "these my own unworthy
weapons; my wand a single limber shoot of ash;

my line tied to its tip; three twisted strands from
the tail of my good grey mare, and my two great
bouncing bumbles fashioned by these fingers from
the hackles of my old game-cock that died gloriously
in Will Andrews' pit a sennight come Tuesday."
As I looked at the dreadful tackle my heart swelled
with pity for the man. But he had said something
about good sport. Well, there were chub in this
part of the river; he might conceivably have caught
a brace of chub.

"And yet," he went on, "see what I have
taken." As he spoke he unslung his creel, inverted it, and upon the grass there poured a
cascade of trout—fat, golden, ponderous. In-
stinctively I removed my hat. Lunatic or fantastic,
here was my master. "These be a dozen and
three," he said in a satisfied voice. "The others
are above, concealed beneath a bush. These, since
seven of the clock." "The others!" I gasped:
"how many, in Heaven's name?" "Three score
and two," he announced simply. "Look you!"—
he moved the heap of fish with his hand, and dis-
closed a stupendous fish of about 6 lb. weight—
"here is a shapely gentleman. A gladsome time
he gave me, forcing me to cast all twice to the
river. But the floating wand betrayed him. I
rode my pony in to him, and now he is mine!"

"You rode your pony?" "Ay, marry! I'm

not so young as I was, and old Tom has carried
me since noon. He has gone round to stable, for
my turf is not for hooves to tread." " *Your*
turf?" "Ay, marry!" said the old gentleman
carelessly, as he placed the fish back in the creel.
" Hah!" he exclaimed, weighing the thing in his
hand, "I have seen a worse evening's fishing.
Trust me! There is two stone in there, my
master!" As he spoke the strap gave beneath the
inordinate weight of chalk-stream trout, and slipped
through his fingers. The creel fell to earth. I
stooped—for this man was worthy of all reverence
—and picked the thing up, bracing myself uncon-
sciously to lift. My body flew upwards with a
jerk which caused me severe pain, and when I had
recovered from the shock of surprise the creel was
in his hands. In the gathering darkness I must
have failed to take hold of it.

"Sir," he said, " I thank you. And now I will
even wish you a good night's rest, and, an you
angle on the morrow, a fair south wind and a dark
water." So saying he began to move silently
away. " But don't you fish to-morrow?" I cried.
It would be an education to see this angler at
work.

The river mist was thickening fast, and partly
by the faint pallor in the west, which was all that
remained of Midsummer Day, partly by the

golden glow of the moon, now climbing among
the branches of the elms in the close, I could see
his vague but comfortable shape ambling softly
from me. "Let me see you fish to-morrow,"
I called. "Nay, nay!" he replied, his voice
lessened by distance, "not to-morrow, gentle sir;
I must wait my year—my long, long year."
Again I heard the gentle sigh, and with it the
dark shadow that was my acquaintance became
one with the blackness that filled a space between
two ageless yews.

This is not true.

XXX

OF COURSE

PURFLING has caught the two-pound trout which the Blennerhassett tried to steal from me.

I saw him.

He was doing it as I reached the meadow.

But—I had this from Joe, who had it from Purfling himself—it only weighs a pound and a quarter.

What a folly is this atheism!

XXXI

OF THE NAMES OF PICTURES

I HAVE painted a very beautiful picture. It is undoubtedly the most lovely thing I have yet done. Nobody, however rude, could mistake its meaning. A thick belt of trees crosses it from one side to the other. The foreground indubitably slopes downwards to the wood. Beyond, further trees stretch into astonishing distance. There would seem to be one hundred miles of trees. The sky is obviously composed of folded clouds, with glimpses of the ultimate blue between. The foreground alone is dubious. I know what it is because I was there; but I cannot lay my hand on my heart and declare that everybody would guess rightly. Yet I have not spared the ochre and dragon's blood, and there are some cunningly-placed shadows such as large stones or bricks would throw. One thing is quite certain about it. It is a foreground, and I defy my most hyper-critical victim to dispute the assertion.

This picture is so beautiful that it must have a

title.   But again, it is so beautiful that a fit title is very hard to find.   I have been wearying my brain to make one.

Landscape painters, I have always observed, are extraordinarily well-educated men.   Whenever I have had occasion to look into the catalogue of a picture exhibition, I have found that most of the landscapes and seascapes have a few lines of verse attached to them by way of title.   Thus :—

No. 1909.   JOHNSON WILLIAMS.

> For men may come and men may go,
> But I go on for ever.

No. 2846.   CROWLE HARBINGER.

> The curfew tolls the knell of parting day,
> The lowing herd winds slowly o'er the lea,
> The ploughman homewards plods his weary way,
> And leaves the world to darkness and to me.

More, the poetry always fits the picture to admiration.

Now, it is evident that men who are able to do this sort of thing have an astonishing knowledge of their poets.   I can imagine Johnson Williams, for instance, painting away at his little stream while, through his memory, the poesy of rivers, miles of it, millions of gallons of it, passes, until, at a given moment, the lines inevitable present themselves before him and he knows the title found. It can only be thus, by a long-continued and indefatigable process of consideration and reflection, that so perfect a harmony between picture and verse is to be established. For it is impossible to suppose that all these titles can be flukes. Such a thing might happen once or twice. It might chance that, of the twenty or thirty pieces of poetry which I know, one absolutely fitted this picture of mine, this composition of trees and sky and distance. But it does not so chance. I am quite sure that such a subject as I have chosen has inspired several poets, and that their utterances are somewhere to be found. But where? Johnson Williams could tell me. But I do not know Johnson Williams. Not knowing him, and not having his peculiar familiarity with English verse, I am reluctantly compelled to abandon the idea of a poetic title.

But (while I am on this subject) if Johnson Williams causes me to form a low estimate of my own education, what kind of a figure do I cut beside certain lady and other novelists, who find an apt quotation not merely to head each book that they write, but to serve as keynote to each chapter of each book that they write, and not merely from the limited source of English verse, but from the boundless ocean of a World's Literature. Such a range of knowledge is unbearable

for the contemplation of a small spirit like mine.
I can only grovel before it as before a mystery.
The fact that to-day everybody is competent to
write a novel, and does, is often adduced in proof
of the high standard of modern education. But
surely this is nothing to the learning indicated by
these novelists' chapter - headings. And their
prodigality! Here is a first chapter four thousand words long which is concerned with the
meeting of the hero and heroine in a railway
carriage. Nothing whatever is established beyond
this certainly important fact. Both are described.
Paddington Station is also unerringly portrayed,
and the destination of the heroine is indicated.
But with the exit of the train from the terminus
the chapter closes. And with what does it begin?
A passage from the Shi King. If I knew what
the Shi King was it would be enough for me. I
would presume upon no further acquaintance, for
I know my own level and I am not man enough
for that kind of thing. This lady, however, treats
the Shi King with a high hand. Needing an
appropriate quotation for her first chapter, she has
only to reflect for a moment and her complete
knowledge of the Shi King affords her the
absolutely right words. For the next stage of
her story she borrows from Emerson, for the
next from Boulmier (three lines from a virelai),

for the next the Book of the Dead serves her turn, and then Epictetus and Gogol and Drummond of Hawthornden and the Saga of Erik the Red (if there is such a Saga), and Voltaire and Heine and Tasso and Montesquieu (assuredly Montesquieu), and Old Play and Anon.

When I think that I compete with such giantesses!

But I was worrying about a name for my picture.

Some painters, less highly endowed than the others, fall back upon what may be called the pseudo-poetic; that is to say, not having at their command a line or lines of genuine authenticated verse which will describe what they have painted, they take some form of words which ring with a well-established sentimentality, thus—

No. 7.	Evening Shadows.	ARTHUR STRUGGLES.
No. 603.	The Trysting Tree.	ARTHUR STRUGGLES.
No. 9001.	Leafy June.	ARTHUR STRUGGLES.
No. 9002.	The Workhouse Door.	ARTHUR STRUGGLES.

But I am so dull that nothing of the kind occurs to me in connection with my picture. This landscape is bathed, obviously, in bright sunlight. There are a number, a great number of trees in it, but none so outstanding and important that it could be dignified into a special feature, and

certainly none that has the appearance of a tryst-
ing tree, which is always of a peculiar and easily-
recognisable shape. Leafy June would do, had I
not been so unwise as to employ Burnt Sienna
rather generously, which has made the foliage
decidedly autumnal, wherefore I wish the purple
which I have put in the foreground to be taken for
heather in full bloom. And there is no Work-
house in the whole composition.

Again, the least imaginative artists simply give
to their pictures the names of the places they
represent, so—

No. 51.   WUGFRID WESTONHAUGH.
Clapham Common, from the Bandstand.

But this is mere label-writing ill fitting an artist.
I can do as much every time I write an address
for the harp in the harp-case. A beautiful water-
colour is worthy of a better description. But
what? But what?

.   .   .   .   .   .

A Large Number of Trees suggests itself to me.
This is, I think, a new line in titles. It has the
merit, moreover, of giving the beholder a hint,
which perhaps, now that I look at the thing again,
may be of service to him or her.

This is a good idea. It provides me with an
unfailing principle in my choice of titles, and it

will save my friends from the pain of asking certain questions. If beneath a sketch, when I exhibit it, I have written, *Willows, not Haystacks*, those who look at it will be able to concentrate their attention wholly on the treatment and other technical qualities. Their minds will be distracted by no doubts as to its general significance. Again, the words, *A Beech in a Grass Field*, legibly inscribed, under the study which I showed to Mrs. Slattery the other day, will put the species of tree and the nature of the ground which I have drawn, beyond question. I shall no longer have to explain the absence of reflection. Nor will Slattery cry out, "Oh, come! That's not bad of our pig-stye," when I am showing him my monochrome of the church.

XXXII

OF TWO MISCREANTS

A S I came along the withy bed to the wooden bridge to-night for a last look north-west-ward, I encountered a dim young woman, who stood in an attitude of extraordinary alertness, grasping a butterfly net and peering determinedly into the profundities of a hedge. Even as I reached her she made a clever little sweep with her weapon, and, holding it up against the exquisite spectacle beyond the downs, uttered a little satisfied noise and got out the killing bottle. On the bridge stood a man, a shortish man, in a soft hat, smoking a cigarette ; he, too, carried the odious muslin bag. A pair of bicycles —male and female—assisted at the sorry sport, leaning, bored, against a rail. These entomologists, having smeared all the posts in the vicinity with a boiled mixture of treacle, brewing sugar, and essence of jargonel pear, were now filling in their time (until it grew dark enough for the Noctuas to come to the horrid bait) in netting such slow-flying Geometers as had the misfortune to cross their path.

I fell into talk with them, found them civil and, the man at any rate, most willing to speak of his hobby. He had marked the withy bed, it appeared, when passing one day, as a likely place for the Red Underwing, an insect which, he bade me note, looked very fine on the sugar. I refrained from saying that it would certainly look finer there than in his cursed cabinet, with a pin through its thorax and its wings set out stiffly at the correct entomological angle. It never does any good to be offensive. This man was a respectable citizen—one couldn't doubt it after looking for one moment on his short side-whiskers, his feeble moustache, his pince-nez and his pear-shaped head. He would be a teacher in a board school, or a grocer in a small way. He might even sell old furniture, or keep a little bookshop. But he had been a schoolmaster at one time of his life, I swear it. His particular manner is only acquired in one trade—and it never loses its hold on a man. Yes, it would have been a mistake to insult him. We are all vicious in spots, and because this admirable husband (he looked too careful to be a father) gave way to moth-killing, who was I (with a rod in my hand) to take him to task. He would only have grown pink, dignified, and hostile. But he would not have stopped treacling. Therefore I was friendly, offered a cigarette, which was accepted with the air of conferring a favour, and drew him out upon his hateful amusements.

His collection of butterflies was practically complete, it appeared. No, he had only been at it five years, but this part of the country was exceptionally rich in lepidoptera. He was quite modest about his success. The wife—as you might say, the cook—she was at his elbow, but he spoke of her as if she were in the other hemisphere —had helped him. As he spoke I became aware that the said wife was moving anxiously about in front of me, net in hand, and, following the direction of her eagle gaze, which darted hither and thither from one side to the other of my own head, I perceived a dusky shape, a moth, that fluttered against the sky. The lust of capture shone in the woman's eye. Her mouth was tense with its suppression, for she knew that the usages of polite society forbid the moth-netting of un-known men. Yet the prospect of the insect escaping was agonising to her. I courteously moved aside. The net swooped. She retired in the direction of the death-bottle.

Yes, the wife was very keen, very keen. She had, that evening, taken—taken, not caught, is the word—*emarginata*. It was she who last summer discovered the Marbled Whites in a certain little wood on the Isle of Wight. Between them they had murdered—taken, I should say—over fifty of those delicate creatures. No, I was not at all inconveniencing them. They had nothing to do now but wait until it was dark enough to visit the sugar. I thought of them, going round with their lanterns and cyanide of potassium, bottling the Red Underwings, and bottling them, and bottling them, and I wondered if it could ever be dark enough for such work.

Did you ever see a Red Underwing? A robust and noble insect: great grey and black wings above, and below bright cherry slashed with black. The bold splendour of the creature, when it is fresh from its pupa-shell, takes away your breath. It is a big chief of the Noctuas, rivalled by few, outshone by none. Among the Hawk Moths alone you shall look for its master. And my decent acquaintance confessed, without a tremor, to having stifled, three nights previously, fifteen of these joyful lives. He and the wife were late to bed that night, " But," he said, " after a long evening out of doors, how soundly one sleeps ! "

Yes, it was surprising how many people collected nowadays. When he began, five years before— (accursed day !)—so general was the amusement which his net excited that he was quite nervous about carrying it. " Bug Hunter ! " they called after him. (No doubt he would grow pink and pretend not to hear, going on with head high.) But now nobody noticed the net, and wherever one went one found someone with whom to exchange information and specimens—or, should one say swop confidences and corpses?

Yes, there were fewer lepidoptera than formerly. The common things that nobody wanted would always abound, but undoubtedly the time was not far off when the rarer kinds would be worked out. He announced the approach of this frightful catastrophe with the absolute certitude of Jonah crying the destruction of Nineveh, but without any visible emotion. Yet there was a certain sadness in his voice, as if he contemplated the disappearance from England of those rarer kinds regretfully (for the good hunting), but fortified by the knowledge that he would be in at the death. Though every moth should become extinct, nothing could ever rob him of the memory of, for example, fifteen Red Underwings slain on a July night in the year now current.

The fact was, he went on, that nobody was content with the number they had of any given insect. It was always possible to make a series more complete, whether by more perfect individuals, or by a wider range of variety. The Silver Washed Fritillary, now. There was a butterfly, now, that was very hard to take in perfect condition. The brambles among which they fly, knock their wings to pieces. (A Silver Washed Fritillary is on its upper side a ravishing arrangement in sepia, raw sienna, and black. Beneath, it defies description. It's name is the simplest and best.) Yes, the brambles knocked them about. He evidently resented the creation of brambles. He looked forward to his trip to the New Forest, due in a few weeks. The Silver Washed should be out by then. He had only twenty, and very few varieties. He seemed to lick his lips. Speaking of Fritillaries, last year he took the Duke of Burgundy (this is one of those adorable little butterflies which will presently be worked out). Seventeen he and his friend had in half an hour. And though they returned again and again to the spot, they never saw another. I suppose they were, as far as that place is concerned, worked out.

He complained that the White Admirals were getting scarcer each year. Now God, when He made the underside of the White Admiral, took His colours from the utterly lovely dawn which must have ushered in the sixth day of Creation. And the Little Blue (a tiny bit of the sky, murderers !)—he hadn't seen a Little Blue for three years. The last time he encountered it—rising all round him they were—he took thirty. Thirty

Little Blues ! There is a special Hell for this man and his fellows.

I left him and the wife and went to another bridge, not far off, and leaning upon the rail I asked myself what in the name of insanity was this man doing, and what in the name of stupidity are we doing to let him do it ? By his own confession this is going on all over the country. There are thousands of these respectable miscreants in our midst steadily " working out " the Duke of Burgundy Fritillary. They dignify their proceedings by the name of Entomology. The boy who robs a bird's nest might call himself an Ornithologist, but that would be no reply to a prosecution under the Wild Birds' Protection Act. Why is a White Admiral less worthy of protection than a golden-crested wren ? It is not for me to say which is the more beautiful of the two.. But if it is thought good to prevent any madman who chooses from going forth in the breeding season to the indiscriminate slaughter of golden-crested wrens and ger-falcons, why do we loose him upon the White Admirals during the short time they have on earth in which to propagate their species ? If Parliament cannot contemplate a birdless England, with what drug—save that of unthinkingness—does it blind its eyes to an England without butterflies and without moths ?

XXXIII

OF AN ESSENTIAL FALSITY

IT is very often difficult to recognise the original in a product of cultivation. A prize pug is about as like a primitive dog as it is like a brontosaurus. Similarly a chalk-stream angler differs incredibly from the barbarian who with a paddle digs mud fish out of South African slime. Yet had man never imagined the eating of fishes, and set about procuring them in some such direct and practical fashion, the Itchen would not rent to-day at £2000 a mile. Or is it to-morrow?

During his journey from the shores of remote antiquity the angler has changed more than his costume and his tackle. He has developed a new point of view, which differentiates him from his old self far more completely than the split-cane and gossamer gut which he wags so dexterously back and forth over his chosen waters. He no longer fishes to eat; rather it may be said he eats to fish. Angling has become a sport, an art, a theory, a rule of life, and its original purpose is wholly obscured. Such carcases as its success-

ful exponent may carry away from the stream
he bestows upon the deserving poor or distributes
as graceful compliments by post among his last
winter's hostesses.   It is fashionable to despise the
flesh of trouts. "After," your more pernicious
kind of angler will say, " I have weighed my fish,
or grassed him, or fairly hooked him, or risen him "
—his choice among these moments depending on
the stage of refinement to which he has advanced
—" I have no further interest in him.   As for
eating him, Heaven forbid !   Give me a cod steak
and oyster sauce."

Like so much of what is said nowadays, this
kind of talk is extremely artificial.   It is born of
long purses and full stomachs.   Civilisation is
made up of such things.   We have to get to grips
with nature to discover their essential falsity.   All
this clothing of sportsmanship, entomology, phren-
ology, contemplativeness, gentleness, and even
humour, in which we have learned to dress up
fishing cannot serve to conceal from the penetra-
ting eye the original simple, sincere attempt of
the carnivorous animal to fill his belly.

My wife appeared with a white face, one hand
flung forth despairingly, a telegram clutched in it.
"Those men," she said, meaning Chavender and
Wickham, whom again we expected, "will be
here at half-past six—not half-past nine, as they

wrote." I said, "Capital! Three hours to the
good." "You don't understand," she said. "They
were to come on the dining-train, and you never
saw such a chicken as has been sent—a misery."
It was my turn to grow pale. "We must
buy more chickens," I said; "several more."
"There are no more," said my wife tragically;
"the village is empty of chickens." I perceived
that my choice lay between a ten-mile bicycle ride
and a little angling. It was not a hard one to
make. "I will catch a trout," I said easily, as
I rose from my chair and began to pull on my
waders. "Let us have tea at once." "Do you
think," she said, "that you had better wait for
tea? It is frightfully important." Her evident
anxiety that I should have every possible minute
for my fishing annoyed me. I said, "I will go
without tea. Though I lack, I will feed your
guests." This I said to show my wife that she
valued the comfort of our guests above mine,
which was false, and that I proposed to supple-
ment her shortcomings, which was base. I
plucked my rod from the lawn and strode forth
to catch our dinner.

It was half-past four o'clock. About five I
anticipated the hatch of red quill customary on
this water in this month at that hour. Meanwhile
I went up the backwater, there haply to dape

a trout. Daping is an absorbing business. Half-past five o'clock (to my annoyance) struck on the church clock, and I had daped nothing. I was not altogether surprised, hardly disappointed (for the rewards of daping are not frequent), in no wise cast down. I rejoined the river and waited for the red quills.

After I had been thus occupied for twenty or thirty minutes our purist Purfling came down stream towards me through the meadow, and, in reply to my question if any fly was showing up the water, informed me that the hatch of red quills was over. It had begun, he said, about half-past four. As it was ended, and as he had caught his (the assumption underlying the pronoun was intolerable) brace, he was going home. He dwelt at some distance from the river.

" I wonder," he said, " if you would do me a favour ? I am a little late and take my road here. There is an old lady at the village—Mrs. Pescod, at the little shop. Hers is the only house at which, this season, I have not left a fish." I exclaimed at his generosity, no less than at his good fortune and skill (the paltry braggart !). " Nay," said he (he always says " Nay "), " there is no merit in giving away what one does not like. I think trout poor stuff. Give me a cod steak and oysters. As for my success I do not com-

plain. But if you will leave these fish with Mrs.
Pescod from me I shall be very grateful. It will
save me ten minutes." I agreed to distribute
his favours for him. I did not see why Mrs. Pescod
should go without trout because I resented his
monstrous request. You will recollect, perhaps,
that I had missed the rise by which he had profited. No decent man in his position could have
suggested to a man in mine the cartage of his
successes. But I hope I do not need to labour
this point.

Purfling went away, leaving in my creel two
noble trout of about 2 lb. each. The fellow can
surely fish.

Mrs. Pescod's supper was provided, but the
dinner of my wife, two hungry fellows, and myself (and I had had no tea) still consisted of
a meagre chicken. It behoved me to bestir myself.

I bestirred myself accordingly—as far as the
run below the mill pool, which I reached by half-
past six. At this time, I knew, Chavender and
Wickham must be already in the house, or at
any rate approaching it with frightful velocity.
On my way I had risen and failed to catch one
young grayling. The surface of the run below
the mill pool remained unbroken during the
five anxious minutes which I spent in scanning

it. The mill pool has only once in my experience of it been wholly devoid of rises. This was the occasion. By this time my hunger was enormous. I thought of that chicken. I thought of the four miserable portions into which I could divide it. I thought of its wretched little legs vanishing in three bites of those strong, ravenous jaws that I had bidden all the way from London to its consumption. I thought of our poor housekeeper reduced to buttered eggs. I thought of a great wheaten loaf there was in the larder. And of myself, I thought of myself. I would be host, I would be carver. Whoever was going to be fed it could not be I—unless I caught a trout within the next half-hour.

It was now that the fancy dress of angling suddenly fell away from it, and I knew it for the stark, grim, elemental business it is. I began to think of the fat fishes which inhabit the mill pool in quite unfamiliar terms. They were no longer the ministers of my pleasure. They were no longer there to afford me the opportunity of exhibiting my sportsmanship, my skill in overcoming drag, my capacity to cheat a cross wind, my ability to cock a fly, my cunning in persuading them among the weed beds. They presented themselves to my imagination as pounds of meat, sizzling morsels of pink flesh, builders up of the system, necessities of life, pang-stayers. The shackles of civilisation became green withes to bind the Samson of animalism. Under the compelling influence of the law, Nature abhors a vacuum, I knotted on a huge alder and combed the pool—wet.

．　　．　　．　　．　　．　　．

Somewhere in one of my boxes was a Silver Doctor.

．　　．　　．　　．　　．　　．

On a water where pike occasionally appear a wagtail spinner is a legitimate item in the dry-fly angler's outfit.

．　　．　　．　　．　　．　　．

In the miller's garden was a manure heap. It was full of brandlings. I began to strip the dressing from a hook.

．　　．　　．　　．　　．　　．

But the clock struck seven, to save me from crime. In half an hour dinner would be served.

"If," I said violently, as I threw hook and brandling from me, "anybody thinks that I am going to dine off a pope's nose with 4 lb. of trout in my basket, he is mistaken—profoundly mistaken." I went home. In spite of my conviction that nature, ultimate judge, was with me, I wore a hang-dog air as I slunk past Mrs. Pescod's cottage. She and her three little orphan grand-children called out "Good evening" to me and waved their hands. I hurried from the presence of this widow and these fatherless. So does civilisation take the pith out of the natural man.

And you would never believe the trouble that Chavender and Wickham and I met with next day in getting two brace of trout for Mrs. Pescod—one from Purfling and one from us. The good woman nearly fell down dead from sheer joy. And my wife (being deceived) was pleased with me. And we were all filled. And Purfling is under an obligation to me. And confession is good for the soul.

. . . . . .

And, while I am confessing, let me say that Chavender caught three and Wickham one of those four fishes.

XXXIV

OF AN ONLY CHUB

THIS morning, on my way to the water, I met James, son of Joe, aged eighteen, gardener, coachman, boot-cleaner, knife-polisher, chicken-master, duck-expert, bacon-raiser, dog-herd, glazier, locksmith, and joiner, to my friend Slattery. James, son of Joe, reminds me of a certain knife which I never owned. It was sold over my head out of its shop-window—so splendid was this knife that it seemed to possess its environment as certain men seem to possess the hotels and railway carriages in which they magnificently dine or superbly sit—it was sold, I say, over my head, by the mercenery brute—King was his name, a vile name—of whose stock it was the glory, to some person or persons (probably a syndicate) furnished with the impossible sum of money which was marked upon it. That knife was suitable for everything. The Pioneer was its name. It would open champagne bottles (I have often handled it), it would draw corks, it would clean, ay! and file finger-nails. It had, cunningly dissembled in the handle, a pair of small folding-scissors, admirably adapted to embroidery work. There was really nothing to which a Pioneer would wish to turn his hand for which, with this knife, he would find himself unequipped. With the large blade, for instance, the felling of timber would have been the merest child's play. There was a tree near my home which I often in those days measured with my eye while waiting for that amount of money, which alone would satisfy the exorbitant King, to come my way. It was a pine tree of which the best log cabins are made. But the knife went otherwhere, and in consequence the pine tree still stands.

In like manner with this knife (with his father indeed—for here surely is heredity at work) James, son of Joe, is suitable for everything and competent in every sphere. Of his age, he is the most remarkable person alive. He has, however, one defect. He knows nothing about fish. Nothing whatever. I will prove it.

This morning he informed me with delight— for he loves me, I think—that a great trout lie by wooden bridge. He measured preposterous lengths on his arm, and finally decided on the distance between his finger-tip and three inches below his shoulder-blade. James, his arms are long, and it was clear to me that in the matter of

Q

this trout, the truth was not in him. But after slaying a fish of half his measurements, I should have been delirious for a month. Therefore I obtained further and better particulars, not of the trout's size, but of its situation, and thus furnished, after bestowing a smile upon James, son of Joe, I approached the lair of this prodigy.

On peering over the bridge rail, as suggested by James, I perceived a chub of about three pounds weight lying in the water.

I thought that I had known every fish in this piece of the river, but I was mistaken. Hitherto our chevin has escaped my vigilance. But he is certainly the only one of his breed in the neighbourhood. Pike we have, a few, eels abound in certain places, crayfish are found on the drag-net in September, of minnows we have the finest head of any water in England, and there are dace and roach. But we have never previously got down to chevins.

It would of course be impossible for me to catch this creature. First of all I could not, for I am not sufficiently crafty. But this entirely apart, it would be a gross error even to angle for him. To throw a fly or flies to our chevin (I have no chub-flies) would be to do that thing which of all others he most ardently desires. For to be taken for a trout, that is the chevin's ambition.

You sometimes see in Regent Street and other places where people congregate, the deck of the *Clacton Belle* let us say, or the Paddock at Ascot, you sometimes see in such places a man who causes you to start and look more closely at him. Then you perceive that it is *not* the present Emperor of Germany, nor William Shakespeare, nor some other person of features easy to be recognised. You see that it is one of those people born alike with an uncommon physiognomy and an incredible nature, who seek by emphasising their natural disadvantages to draw to themselves the eyes of the multitude.   It is as unfortunate to be given a face which resembles William Shakespeare's as to have a port-wine mark.   Each is a target for the stares of those who pass one in the street, and that kind of notice should be painful to a man. If by his extraordinary energy and moderate abilities he has won himself a place in the world's estimation which renders his features familiar to the public, he has perhaps a right to feel some satisfaction when people's eyes fill with interest at his approach. He has earned this doubtful delight.   But if it is merely his physical attributes which cause them to gape and turn round and nearly get run over by the Chelsea omnibus, I say that he has no title whatever to congratulate himself. Let the stares be complimentary or pitying or merely derisive, it

is all one. The fellow is an object of false curiosity
and his position should be detestable to him. But
is it? In the case of the man with a port-wine
mark probably, in the case of the hunchback
possibly, but in the case of the mock celebrity,
not at all. He revels in it. The nudge that goes
between the oncoming couple never escapes him.
He is on the look out for it. His wife will tell
you how often people have remarked Andrew's
resemblance to Napoleon with almost as much
pride as if she had been married to that scourge
of humanity. He goes to all the fancy dress balls
there are in the costume appropriate to his unfortunate condition, and the murmurs of surprise
which follow his triumphant progress about the
rooms are sweeter to his ears than the whispers of
love.

And in his ordinary clothes, should he be an
imitation of Nelson, or Lord Charles Beresford,
he rolls seamanlike; if the Duke of Wellington is
his model he makes every inch of him try to look
martial, yea! though he cheapen bananas on a
barrow. He shaves his beard, not because he
is cleaner so, but because Mr. George Alexander
has particular views about his hair. And surely
there is no wilder folly than to do any particular
thing solely because someone else has done it
before you. What may be highly convenient if

one is an actor-manager with a fine chin, may be
suicidal for a gentleman in the City with a tendency
to bronchitis.   But though he nearly lose his life
in the winter, with the spring and his first saunter
down St. James's Street, he is amply repaid if one
eye dilates, and he hastens with quickened pulse
in the direction of his prototype's theatre, doing
his best to look as if he were late for rehearsal.

Such is the chevin in a trout stream.

I say nothing about him in his own place.
Where dace and roach excite the emulous pole-
fisher, where barbel growt after macaroni-and-cheese
at dawn, where perch pull gay floats down among
the water lilies, there the chevin is all very well.
Fair play to him he is no easy fish to catch, though
why anyone should wish to catch him I cannot
conceive.   His play is contemptible, for his heart is
dead within him from the strike, and he is only fit
for pike to eat, though they do not think so.

But in trout water he is out of his class, and,
like every other thing which gets really above
its proper sphere, he is miserable unless he can
impose himself on the world as one who is there
of right.   Should he do this he is happier than he
could ever be among fishes of his own or slightly
better kidney.   In water where chevins abound
and trout are rarities no one would mistake the
logger-headed creature for anything but himself.

So, in such waters, he never receives the compliment for which his snobbish soul craves. But where trout and grayling of three to four pounds are fairly common possibilities, your plump chevin, well dissimulated in a deep place, may easily pass for a sporting and desirable fish. Then, like the mock Alexander after that encounter in St. James's Street, he is well content, and if an angler should take him seriously and offer him a cocked dun he has to put a fearful force upon himself to refrain from rising to it. How he boasts to the daces afterwards.

It has now become my duty to expose this impostor. The other rods must know, and any visitor who comes to fish, that the vicinity of the wooden bridge is polluted. Purfling I am tempted to send after " a great trout that defies all my skill." His subsequently expressed pity for my ignorance would be of a delicate savour. But no. Purfling must be told like the rest. It would be injudicious to send Purfling after a chevin.

There is no saying what kind of a seizure would carry him off, and I do not desire Purfling's death. His pity I could bear but not his obituary notices. And, away from the river, I believe him to be a useful citizen. He addresses meetings (I am told), and it is well that meetings should be addressed.

Otherwise they would wreck halls, and all destruction of property is to be deprecated. Therefore Purfling, by saving the halls from destruction, plays a useful part, and there are too few useful men. I too am a useful man. By abstaining from addressing meetings I too save halls from destruction. For all these reasons I will spare Purfling.

The chevin then is, and shall be further, unmasked. James Lavender shall be told and everybody else. I will spread it about. I will tell the men who touch their hats when we meet in the village of an evening. Instead of saying " A fine night" or "a wet evening" I will say "There is a chevin by the bridge. Tell it out." So the thing shall be known to all users of the bridge. I would, were I competent in lettering, inscribe a signboard thus—" It is only a chevin," and set it up on the bridge end. But I cannot letter nicely and I must depend on the mouth-to-mouth method. James, son of Joe, and others who go that way will in future look over-rail upon a chevin and will know what they see. And they will spit upon the chevin. If they do not I will pay them till they do. And the chevin will know himself unmasked and the envious blood of him will turn black with rage, and he will float belly up, and the shrimp will eat him.

Or—for a chevin is tenacious of purpose—he will shrink from public observation and will only show himself to the little children who sometimes play there, hopeful of their ignorant admiration. But I shall tell the children too.

Thus after a time he will learn the futility of his conduct and go away down or up stream whence he came, where other chevins are. There he will excite the cupidity of chevin fishers, but he will do it on his own merits. I trust that the lesson will sink in and that for the future he will content himself with being known for a moderate chevin rather than being mistaken for an impressive trout.

XXXV

OF GRAYLINGS, LARGE AND SMALL

I AM in the third day of a snuffling cold.
It is raining. It always has been raining.
It will always rain. Out on the road a child (a
Bunting grandchild or great-grandchild, I think)
runs backwards and forwards, making a noise like
the baby of a locomotive.

I stand in need of a shave. I am a failure. I
have no friends. I do not want to go out and
fish and my wife will not let me. I cannot taste
the tobacco I am smoking. Perhaps I should say
that I can taste it and that it is very nauseous.
I have to force myself to smoke it.

I will write about graylings.

I will most venomously abuse them.

There are two kinds of grayling, big graylings,
and little graylings. And first, of the big kind.

The big graylings, then, rise best during those
months when it is unlawful to kill them. In June
you will catch many big graylings on the May-fly
you throw for trout. When you have hooked
them they take an enormous time to tire out and

land. Landed, they take an eternity to un-
hook.

Some liar once said that the grayling has a
tender mouth. Everyone who has since treated
of this fish has repeated the lie. I shall not. The
grayling has a mouth like an umbrella ring. Once
your hook is embedded there it is almost impossible to get it out. By the time you have got it
out the grayling is practically dead. But not
absolutely. If she were, there would be comparatively little to worry you. You would only
have a grayling on your conscience.

But it is June.

It becomes necessary to restore your grayling
to life.

Therefore, while the great trouts rise all about
you, gulping down the May-flies, you grovel on
your belly, and nurse your capture back to consciousness.

You hold her head up stream and you wave her
about in the water for several minutes, while she
moves her mouth and her gills slowly, deliberately.
Then you let her go. Instantly she turns upside
down and begins to float away. Her eye meets
yours glassily, reproachfully. Her martyred air
distracts you. You scoop her out with the net
and repeat the performance.

The trouts go on rising busily.

Very likely the grayling weighs three or four pounds—for only at this season do the very largest feed. She is a glorious fish. To exhibit such a fish at the end of the day would, in September, make your name. In June, however, it would cover you with infamy. Of this the grayling is perfectly well aware.

She is quite comfortable. She knows herself safe. She is in no hurry. You cannot leave her. She prolongs the experience, slowly moving her mouth, slowly opening and closing her gills.

If you were not a fool and a sportsman you would beat her on the skull and throw her in a bed of nettles. If you were Blennerhassett you would call her an out-of-condition trout.

But you prop her up between two reeds.

Deliberately she turns over.

The trout go on rising.

At last she finds the fun begin to pall, and with a sluggish movement slips from between your hands and sinks to the gravel sulkily. You are free of her.

You now find that the rise of May-fly is over.

The last insect is coming down stream. A large fish takes it. You throw to it. It takes your fly.

It is another grayling.

You may kill graylings from July till February. That sounds very good. Eight months of it. Here, you say, is a fish that should be cultivated. Let us examine this matter.

In July the large graylings disappear. They are not. In August the trout copy their pernicious example. Only the little graylings remain. (I shall deal with them in a moment.)

In September the big graylings emerge from their hiding-places and provide admirable sport. I have nothing but praise for them in September. This is my one good word for the grayling log.

In October my hands become lifeless after they have once been wetted. In November I die if I stand for more than half an hour by a river. In December I stay in London. In January I stay indoors. In February I stay in bed.

A fish which causes me so much annoyance cannot win my pardon by offering me eight months' fishing on these terms. Therefore I object to big graylings, except in September. And this is not September.

And now of little graylings.

The little graylings feed for ever. Yet they never grow up. There are little Peter Pan graylings in this river which have haunted certain spots for eight years. They were in those spots when first I threw a fly on Clere. They will be in those spots when I am dead.   I think they will be the cause of my death, for they irritate me excessively, and nothing shortens a man's life like constant worry.

. The little graylings (as deficient in bowels of compassion as they are in the thyroid department) will not care.   They will go on rising and feeding and fooling about, pretending to be large fishes, just as happily, just as stupidly, though I am not there to be maddened by them.   They will never give me a thought in my cold grave, where they will have placed me.   They have no thoughts.

There is a pool on this river.   We call it the Island Pool.   It is very deep and I have been frightened by the fishes that I have seen in it. The little graylings are not frightened by them. They have not brains enough to be frightened by anything.   Not even by me.   They rise eternally in this pool.   The water and trees are so arranged that it is impossible to tell from below what manner of fish has caused any given break in the surface.   The little graylings know this. They have lived so long in this pool that they have managed to acquire this one piece of knowledge.   It moulds their whole existence.   Morning, afternoon, and evening (and at night for all I know) they rise and rise in the hope that I shall see them and cast to them.   They rise at nothing

at all. This they do that I may imagine the
beginnings of a hatch. They are malicious little
things.

When I see them I cast to them, because I do
not know for certain that they are not large trouts.
Then they are delighted, and dash off giggling to
tell the big fish about me.

I hate them.

.   .   .   .   .   .

It is impossible to teach little graylings wisdom.
There is one that I am always catching. I caught
her six times the week before last. On the Monday
and Tuesday once, on the Thursday twice, and on
the Friday three times. I find that this makes
seven occasions on which, in that one week, I
dragged this same miserable little fish out on to
the bank. It doesn't matter. It would be all the
same to that little grayling if I had snared her
seventeen times, yes, or seventy. Last week I
killed her eight times, but without any effect upon
her. She is still there.

If I could see the creature, perhaps I might
avoid her. But she is invisible. A little grayling
in fast water is as inconspicuous as a Marconigram
as it throbs across the ether. Even could I locate
this fish I doubt if I should be able to elude her,
because she moves with intense rapidity.

In the run which she infests there is a tremendous trout. He is always there. I cannot drive him away. He is that kind of trout. Now and then he takes a fly. He never takes mine. That is the sort of trout he is. He amuses himself at my expense.

Very well.

I arrive within casting distance of this humorist. I cast. The little grayling hurls herself upon my fly. She is without reverence or fear. The great trout cannot inspire her with awe. The smack of my fly upon the water cannot alarm her. Because I am half blind and hope that the trout has risen, I strike, and the little grayling is somewhere in the meadow. I detach her from my hook with infinite trouble, place her in the water and cast again. The little grayling is already waiting to receive my fly.

I fancy that she is subsidised by the trout to annoy me.

You have no conception of the irritation that this little grayling causes me.

To-morrow I shall torture her.

.   .   .   .   .   .

Generally, then, of these little graylings, I will say this. They are the most contemptible of fishes. They are deceivers, raisers of false hopes, liars.

They are nincompoops and popinjays and niddings. They are all levity and sham, masqueraders, infirm of purpose, gluttonous, heart-breaking, effervescent, undesired, conspiring, omnipresent, ignorant, unspeakable.

And I will say this . . .

No, I will say this.

They make good fishing an irritation and they make bad fishing unbearable. When three fishes, not to be seen, are rising at the same time and you cast to one of them, the other two are good trout. That which you hook is a little grayling —which has just enough strength to dart about sufficiently to scare the two trout. When at last you come to Crab Hatch and throw to the fat fish that shows you his head and his tail once a minute on the glide, it is a little grayling that you pull out. When you step cautiously into some shallow backwater, by which manœuvre alone you shall approach three or four of the largest trout that you have ever seen, it is a little grayling which streaks upstream from between your waders and gives the office (as is said) to his betters.

For the little grayling is by nature a darter-about, an uneasy, tattling, common informer, a comer between a man and his amusements, a kill-joy, a spoil-sport, a breeder of mistrust, a bell-man, a scare-monger, a yellow-journalist, a moor-hen. She is a small-minded fish, a riser-at-nothing, a mere breaker of surfaces, a ring-producer, a maker of deceptive sounds, a frog. A jelly-fish is a better fish. I had rather see a dog fetching sticks than a little grayling at play on a good gravel. She is as distressing to me as a Candidate's child that lisps the praises of his dada to a mass meeting. Politics is a man's job. Rising is the business of large earnest fishes. If the little grayling came up in search of food I might have more respect for her. But she doesn't. The less there is on the water the more eagerly does she rise, which is absurd.

The anguish of a blank day is considerable, but it is tenfold keener if at every odd moment one has been tricked into supposing that the fly was coming on. That is the little grayling's idea of giving one a pleasant time.

It is one which she shares with the daces alone. With the daces !

No other fishes do this. Salmon do not ; pike do not. Who has ever seen crayfishes messing about after nothing at all, on top of all the best glides ? Do carps do it ? No. Perches ? No. Roaches ? I don't know. Perhaps. Add them, if you will, to the others. A precious trinity. Barbels ? Do they do it ? No. They live on barbel baits, which they suck from anglers' hooks

R

far down in the water. Do chubs? No. Not even chubs do this thing. What chubs despise the little graylings do.

I can say nothing worse about the little graylings.

Where is the eucalyptus?

XXXVI

OF A FLEDGLING

WE sat in the big garden-window, she darning my socks or polishing her nails, in either case like a good wife; I reading aloud after my commendable practice. Presently I became aware of insistent competition; a shrill, tiny sound was interrupting me. I cannot bear interruption. I desisted, laid the book down, and sought the origin of this impertinence. After a time I perceived it. On the path hopped a fledgling, fallen, like Lucifer, through pride. It had thought to fly when it was only fit to hop. I can imagine it, goodliest of the brood, lording it in the matter of elbow-room and getting more than its fair share of worm. And this afternoon, sated with such easy triumphs, it had said to the others (the parents being for the moment away), "Now, you scum, just watch me fly like the governor and mater." So here it was, on the path, hopping and proclaiming its wrongs to the garden. For one cannot suppose that its spirit was at all chastened by experience. It was obviously in a very bad temper, and if there was one thing it hated and despised it was the air. A more tricky, unsubstantial stuff it had never, in all its days, encountered. Rotten! that was the word for it.

It stretched its scrawny little neck; it seemed to stand on tiptoe in order to be heard the better. Not a doubt but it was seriously concerned about itself, and very angry with its parents. These, from neighbouring bushes, their voices harsh with emotion, shrieked reproof, advice, gloomy prophecy. The young one piped his sauce back at them from the ground-level.

" Oh! " the mother was crying, very probably. " Oh! naughty child. I told you not to, you know I did. How could you be so wilful and headstrong? This will break my heart."

" Bother your heart," the chick seemed to make answer. " I've pretty near broke my neck. What a thud! And it's all your fault, going away and leaving me like that! "

Then the old cock would scream: " Don't you dare to answer your mother so. I won't have it, do you hear? Conceited little fool! I've no patience with you. Look what a trouble you're causing us. You and your half-inch wings!" He spread his own ample pinions and flew gracefully to another bush.

" That's right "—from the chick. " Show off, do. If you'd talked a little less about the ease of flying, I shouldn't be here. And now, what are you going to do about it? I can't go on like this. It's precious cold and you know my chest isn't strong. And it looks like rain, and I'm starving. Hang it! can't you do something, one of you? "

" Get under a leaf," begged the mother. " And come away from that man and woman. I can't feed you while they're about."

" A pretty mother, you are! Where's your maternal instinct? Frightened of these two people, are you? Well I'm not. They look all right. I'll *show* you."

He swaggered insolently towards my wife's foot with intimidating cries. She moved it that he might advance.

" There! What did I say? The woman can't face *me*."

" The cat," shrieked the mother, " the yellow cat'll get you. I always said you'd come to a bad end."

" So did I." This was from the father. I think the memory comforted him.

The mention of the yellow cat set me thinking. Hitherto I had been content to listen to what they were saying, for it was so essentially of the situation. Now it seemed to be getting time to act. This yellow cat is an evil beast. Continually when I step into the garden I catch, out of the corner of my eye, a glimpse of its tawny hinderlands vanishing over the wall. It fears me because I throw stones at it, though Heaven knows it need have no fear. I am not dexterous with pebbles. But I always throw them in the yellow cat's direction, because I am a man and have a right to throw stones at cats, and this cat is the only evil thing in Willows. It wakes me, sweating, out of sweet sleep. Its colours clash. And it eats birds. I have every reason to detest it. Moreover I do.

I vowed therefore that the yellow cat should not eat this little braggart that hopped, high-piping, among our feet. Conceit is of youth. It would be poor behaviour to condemn the small misery to the yellow cat, because it had thought too highly of itself. Here was an adventurer, an explorer, a sort of fledgling Lieutenant Shackleton. Conceit is also of enterprise. Without it no one would innovate anything. One has to have a pretty good opinion of oneself before one steps off the beaten track. The very action is a self-confident one. But we do not think Lieutenant Shackleton conceited. We call him a fine fellow and stand him dinner.

I decided to stand the fledgling dinner, ay! and bed and breakfast, till his sprouting wings should grow strong enough to carry him away from the yellow cat.

I acquired the fledgling,—his parents cursing me, but they misunderstood my motives—and cast about for a receptacle ; a lodging, not a cage. The birdlet's safety demanded something of the sort. My eye met, my reason rejected, several things— A cigarette-box, a glass-fronted cabinet, a string-bag. The creature meanwhile lay, still but palpitating, in my palm, its callow beak resting against a finger, its eyes closed in the extremity of terror. It was utterly dissatisfied with its situation.

I selected my fishing-creel. This was the very thing ; large, deep, well ventilated, of dim interior. In it I lodged our guest.

I took dry grass, improvised a cosy nest, induced the fledgling to sit there. I closed the lid. Hospitality demanded that food should be provided.

I bethought me that young birds like worms, that worms are their staple fare. I took my very large clasp-knife and went into the garden where I procured two worms, pink, luscious, entirely suitable for a fledgling.

I introduced the worms into the creel. I found that the fledgling had deserted the nest I had made for it, was striving to break out through the wicker, a manifest impossibility. Mine is a strong creel, fifteen years old. It bears me while I meditate by the banks of rivers, and my thoughts alone are no light weight. I restored the fledgling to the nest, added the worms, and went for further food.

I procured a saucer, brown bread, milk. I steeped the crumb of the bread in the milk. I brought sugar, one lump, and therewith sweetened the mess. Sugar is sustaining. The German army performs prodigies of route-marching on sugar alone. I placed the saucerful of bread, milk, and sugar in the nest, after replacing the fledgling in that snug nook. The worms, too, had wandered away. These I placed in the sugar and milk and bread. Then I put the fledgling on the whole and, closing the creel, stole away confident that the bird would do well enough.

Half an hour later I returned.

The fledgling was dead.

This is really a tragedy—one of the innumerable tragedies of good intentions; for I have been told, since, that had I not meddled, the chick would have been cared for by its parents and nursed, out of nest, to a size, strength, and wing-power which should enable it to look after itself. If this be so—which I should like to deny—I am responsible for the death of this young bird. Yet my intentions towards it were of the most kindly. If I sinned it was through ignorance, which is no excuse, hardly a palliation. I assumed a respon-

sibility for which I was unfit. That is the truth
of the matter.

But, had I washed my hands of the affair, had I
left the parent birds and the yellow cat to decide
the fate of the fledgling between them, should I
feel any happier than I do? I trow not.

I wish the little thing, when it tumbled from its
nest, had taken some other road than that which
led it by the garden window. This summer how
many Wiltshire chicks have essayed a too early
flight and perished miserably of cold or at the fangs
of predatory beasts? Who shall say? I know
there must have been many thousands of them.
But the knowledge disturbs me no wit. In the
same way I know that thousands of human babies
die every year because their ignorant fathers and
mothers take insufficient care of them. And I
cannot pretend that I suffer acutely because of
this. But if a child that I loved were among
them——

It is only because the fate of this particular
fledgling was forced on my notice that I am distressed. Being distressed, I feel resentment—but
against whom, against what? The chick? That
were folly. The parent birds? That were worse.
They were getting food for the little thing. They
cannot possibly be blamed. Myself remains. Yet,
knowing nothing of birds, I was on the horns of a

dilemma. I chose that which seemed the least heartless, and my choice resulted in a slow death for my bantling instead of a quick one. For my ignorance of birds, then, I will accept blame, but not for the chick's death. For that nobody seems to be responsible.

XXXVII

OF OBERHAUSEN ON A SEA-STREAM

THE fishes of this river elude me more and more successfully. Perpetually it rains. I cannot angle ; I cannot paint. I propose to boast.

Hitherto I have been absurdly modest. You would suppose from what I have written that I never catch any fishes here. You would be right. But I have caught fishes in my time, great fishes. I am in a mood to dwell upon my blood-stained past. I do this whenever it rains all the week. Let us go to Norway, to that island where I experienced that Perfect Thrill of which I have told you, to that sea-stream where Mac-Alister and I discovered how to catch flounders esoterically.

At full flood this sea-stream is nothing but a shallow lake, a quarter of a mile each way across, with a narrow mouth at each end, the one opening out of the lake above, the other, fifty yards broad, leading almost directly into the Gulf Stream. At the end of the ebb this second mouth might be cleared by an athletic man, properly stimulated, and the shallow lake has become a series of empty pans floored with sand and seaweed among which the sea-stream (you might wet your ankles in it) meanders, clear as crystal and still as glass, save when a flounder wallows across it. I am not a surveyor, and I cannot reach any just approximation—at any rate, not within a million gallons or so—of the amount of water which has to flow out, twice a day, through the sea-gate. But this is a matter of very minor importance, for in flowing out it makes a very pretty, narrow, V-shaped torrent, gliding down to a big, tumbling, foaming pool, where the sea-trout lie, and if Neptune, god of fishes, wills it, go for any standard pattern that you send them.

My first experience of these sea-trout was very painful. I had been casting all morning in a dead calm on the lake, and I had done badly, very badly. There are few games better worth playing than throwing a dry-fly from a boat over rising fish. But when they are not rising and will not be tempted, it is a most dispiriting form of exercise. At two o'clock, I gave it up and went down to the sea-stream to find it tearing through the sea-gate—deep, strong, and foaming. I had never seen it like that before, for hitherto, in my ignorance, I had fished it on the low ebb.

To do myself justice, the Herr Dr. Oberhausen and MacAlister, my good comrades, had done the same, and they are professed sea-trout fishers. Nothing but small finnocks had been caught, and we held the place cheaply. Still, finnocks are better than nothing at all, and it was for finnocks that I hoped that afternoon. I carried a light greenheart. My gut was the same drawn stuff that I had been using on the lake. 1 put on a Yellow Pennell, and cast it into the tumbling water. Tug! A giant fish had me at its mercy. Whir-r-r! The reel screamed. Splash! The great fish left the water. Good-bye! The gut had parted, naturally. My eyes were opened. I soaked a stout cast thoroughly; I bended it to my line. I tied on another Pennell; I threw it in. Tug! Whir-r-r! Splash! as before; but the gut held, and we had at it. The fish did what he pleased with me. In that rush of water he ran out line in the manner of the fabled tarpon. I may have played him for fifteen seconds. Then he went into the seaweed—the bright, golden, tough, abundant seaweed—and then I went in after him and recovered my fly with some difficulty. And there my sport ended for the day, for not another rise had I. This was not to be borne. Next day, rather earlier on the ebb, I was there with a double-handed split-

cane, sixty yards of line, and stout gut. The
sea-stream ran out furiously, and the fish came
bravely. One, two, three, I rose and missed ;
four, I hooked. He jumped and was off. Five,
I landed ; 2½ lb. Six, I hooked, played, and lost.
Seven, I landed ; 2½ lb. Eight and nine, I rose.
The casting was dead into the eye of a bright
sun ; there was no breath of wind, and I sweated
and swore and had the best time of my life.
For these were my first sea-trout. MacAlister
sat on the rocks, smoked, and told me his opinion
of my angling. But I cared very little. The
discovery was made, and we knew when to tackle
the sea-stream in future.

On the morrow MacAlister was set at them
and I went down to receive instruction. Mac-
Alister took off his coat, rolled up his sleeves, lit
a vast pipe, and entered the water. One, two,
three, he rose, hooking and losing one of them.
Four he landed ; 2¾ lb. Five ran out thirty yards
of line making, apparently, for Greenland, across
the Arctic Sea. But MacAlister managed to turn
him, and there they were, fish tugging away
below MacAlister, MacAlister holding on for dear
life, and biting into his pipe-stem deeper and
deeper every moment. The trout had never
shown himself (and I may add, never did show
himself) and this circumstance has led MacAlister,

ever since, to swear that he had to do with the
father of all sea-trout. I gave him advice. I said :
" Come out on to the shore. Bring the fish out of
the fast water. Manœuvre him into that little
bay below you. You must lose him if you let him
hang on like that." MacAlister paid no attention
to me, but pulled at his pipe till the bowl was
ready to crack. After a time he said something
about "too much seaweed," and something about
"interfering fools," and then the fish broke upstream towards him, and his monologue ceased.
He reeled in nimbly, and came out of the water.
When the rod bent again, the fish was in the
weed, and after hope had turned to conviction, and
conviction had become despair, my poor friend
waded in sadly, detached his fly, and set to work
again, only to rise one fish, which he hooked and
lost. I sat on the rocks—smoked, and told
MacAlister my opinion of his angling. Presently,
the tide ran down to a dribble, and we went home.

The Herr Dr. Oberhausen, to whom we related
these things on his return from the slaughter of
ryper, was more than impressed. He exhibited an
intense animation. His eyes grew large and bright.
He swore "by the holy poker" (what fire did it
stir ?), and "by the holy fly " (where did it buzz ?),
and several other objects of interest to the hagio-
grapher, that he would be the death of some of

those fish within twenty-four hours. Even the Adelphi were infected by his enthusiasm, and vowed, by such things as Oberhausen had left uninvoked, to attend the morrow's execution. These Adelphi shared our house, fed with us, played bridge with us, but were not of us. They were in no sense sportsmen. Indeed, their attitude towards all sport was that of Mr. Vandeleur towards Mr. Scrymgeour. They "regarded it with an indifference closely bordering on aversion," and they sought, at meals, to draw us from our talk of fish and tackle into discussion of the great models of English letters. Yet, if the divine spark was kindled for once in their bosoms, who shall say that they came to Norway in vain?

The flood-tide turned. For an hour the sea-stream flowed out calm and deep. Then on the far side a few dimples showed on the surface. This roughness extended, as the depth grew less. Another break came in the near side, lengthened in its turn till it met the first in midstream, and the V began to form. At this moment Oberhausen appeared on the bank, followed at a respectful distance by MacAlister and by me. Then came the Adelphi each with a Great Model under his arm. The spectators took up their positions upon neighbouring rocks, and Oberhausen set to work! I fear that our presence may have daunted him, for he said that in such a sun angling was folly, and affected a reluctance to begin. But when he dropped his flies on to the smooth, gliding surface, a yard from the inner side of the V, out from the foam came a great black fin, inspected the butcher and the red-and-teal, swam all round them, followed them down and across the stream, thought better of it and returned whence it had come. " Did you see that ? " cried Oberhausen. Yes, we had undoubtedly seen that. " It's far too bright," said Oberhausen. We encouraged him to continue. He cast into the broken water, and a fish seized one of his flies with a rush. Oberhausen drove the hook home, ran his fish down into the calmer water, mastered him, netted him, and came to land ; 4 lb.

" A fine fish," said Oberhausen. " Clean run." He pointed with pride to the obscene sea-lice which infested the trout. " I doubt it's too bright," he went on. " Aren't my flies too big ? " " Go into the water," said I, as I poleaxed the fish with the handle of the net. " Go back into the water, and don't waste your breath in such foolishness. Heaven smiles on you. Deserve its smiles. To work ! " The Adelphi now approached. " What is this fish ? " asked Demea. " A pike ? " " Nay," said Micio, " it is a John Dory." And they laughed. They could jest like that in the presence

s

of a clean-run four-pounder. MacAlister and I had hardly laid the fish reverently to rest in the shade of a rock, when we heard Oberhausen's reel singing again. This fish took him far down and over his waders, and MacAlister had to go out to him with the net; 3½ lb. " I doubt," said I, as they came ashore, " I doubt your flies are too big." " Better give it up," said MacAlister. " It's folly to fish in such a sun. You will get no sport, Oberhausen."

But Oberhausen, the moment the hook was released, had bolted up to the top of the sea-stream. He was wasting no time now. Nor did the fish give him much breathing space, for the 3½-pounder was hardly dead ere the learned doctor was doing battle again. This fish plunged into a bed of weed, ran through it, and leaped into the air on the other side. But the gods fought for Oberhausen, the tackle held, and the fish scaled 3½ lb. Oh, sirs ! The very Adelphi warmed up. There was no more talk of pike and John Dory. Perhaps at that moment they realised that there are joys in life which no study of the Great Models, however persistent, may yield. Micio said : " This is magnificent." " He's into another," said Mac-Alister. By this time Oberhausen was working like a machine. He ran his fish down its allotted fifty yards, turned it at the proper point, headed it into the calm little bay aforesaid, gave it the butt, and scooped it out with the net. This fourth fish, however, escaped at the third manual exercise, and the Adelphi lamented aloud, wondering that we cared so little. Of course, with three good fish on the bank, no one would grudge a fourth his life. But the Adelphi lacked experience. What they wanted now was to see the bank strewn with dead fishes. Oberhausen was fishing again. He wanted one more. And in five minutes he got it; $2\frac{1}{2}$ lb. This was the end. The sea-stream had run down to nothing at all, the sea-trout had all gone over the bar into deep water, where fishing was out of the question. Oberhausen, that he might have nothing wherewith to reproach himself, gave it one more turn from top to bottom, and then we loaded up the basket and the net with the four fish ($13\frac{1}{2}$ lb. in all) and set our faces for home, with high resolves for the morrow.

XXXVIII

OF OBERHAUSEN AND A POACHER

I FIND that, after all, it is about the exploits of Oberhausen that I have been boasting rather than my own. No matter. We have at last managed to get some blood—I mean really to splash it about—in this book. I am really very much obliged to my friends. The reader of a book that professes to treat of angling has a right to expect some sport, and had it not been for Chavender and MacArthur and MacAlister and Oberhausen I should have given you, in this respect, very poor value for your money.

While, therefore, we are concerned with Norway, let me (in my gratitude) trumpet the prowess of Oberhausen yet again. I have told you how he catches sea-trout. I propose to tell you how he takes poachers. Now I have never caught a poacher in my life, nor do I know anyone but Oberhausen who has. Here, therefore, I present you a faithful little picture of a Norwegian poaching affray, and if it is not so violent and

murderous as you hope, you must blame the
Norwegian character, not Oberhausen. Nor me.

The rent which MacAlister and Oberhausen
and I paid to the commune of our island was
employed for the good of all the inhabitants.
Our lease was granted by the commune. It
was executed by several of the more important
members of the commune. This is to be noted.

From the first there had been talk of nets.

Mr. Thorwaldsen, in whose house we lived,
had warned us that we might light upon some
of these engines of destruction. I was shocked
to hear this, for I did not know, as did Mr. Thorwaldsen, that the first thought of a Norwegian
peasant on seeing a bit of water is, "How soon
can I put a net through it?" But for ten days
we never saw a sign of a net. Then Oberhausen's
great adventure took place.

I lay at rest upon the bosom of the lake.
Across half a mile of unruffled water I could
see Oberhausen at work, his form silhouetted
against the water of the sea-stream. This was
in the days before we learned how to fish this
place—the finnocky days. His rod flashed in the
pitiless sun as he flailed manfully away. Where
I was no fish moved, for there was no fly on the
water. And yet I went on fishing—dry, sunk,
even trailed—for there were hungry mouths in

the house, and this was the third day of a great
calm. Presently, I secured a largish brown trout
off the mouth of a stream, and at once began
to anticipate a great basket. Across the lake
came a hail. Oberhausen had left the sea-stream.
" Hullo ? " I cried, fishing away with the exaggerated care which a capture in such weather always
engenders. " I have a net," called Oberhausen.
" Break it up," I advised, and went on fishing.
Confound ! I had missed a rise. After that I
was even more careful, and paid no further attention to Oberhausen and his net.

Suddenly my poor friend's voice was raised
upon a different key. There was anger in it,
and a trace of apprehension. " No, no," I could
hear. " You mustn't do that. Keep off." One
glance was enough to show me that Oberhausen
was engaged in battle. I whirled the boat's
head round and set off to his rescue. The
approach of reinforcements seemed to cow the
enemy. There was no more noise of strife.
When I beached the boat, I found we had to do
with a Mr. Henrik Ibsen, member of the committee, a signatory to our leases, one of our land-
lords. The trouble arose from the carelessness of
Mr. Ibsen in leaving his fine new net stretched
across the mouth of the sea-stream till 11 a.m.,
instead of taking it up four hours earlier, as his

custom had hitherto been.   Immunity had made
him reckless.   Greed had grown with success.
And now this painful exposé resulted.   He clung
to a bunch of his net with one hand; with the
other he menaced Oberhausen or appealed to
Heaven indiscriminately.   Oberhausen held on to
the net.   To all Mr. Ibsen's arguments, abuse, and
protestations he made one reply :   " Ikke forstaar "
—" I do not understand," the simple, dignified, all-
sufficing answer of the Briton in difficulties abroad.
As I stepped ashore I heard these words barked
out in Norwegian.   " To blazes with your ikke
forstaar !   Give me my net."   This was his last
effort.   He yielded to superior force ; the net and
a murdered sea-trout of 4 lb. weight which had
spent the night in it were put into the boat, and
while I rowed Oberhausen towards home, where
the cause was to be tried by Mr. Thorwaldsen,
president of the committee, he told me his tale.

He had, it seems, marked the net's corks in the
very entering in of the sea-stream, and as the tide
receded he had been able, by deep, indignant
wading, to secure it.   He had no sooner hauled
it to the lake-side, a matter of half a mile, than
Mr. Ibsen appeared like a whirlwind, demanding
his net shamelessly, swearing at Oberhausen, and
striking him (so manifest was his villainy) on the
chest.   The rest I knew.

The trial was conducted in true Norsk fashion in the open air. The proceedings were extraordinarily public, and everyone who passed along the high road was welcome to attend them, and attended them. In the Lofoten no one is blasé. Public interest was extensively aroused. Before judgment was given, I suppose there were seven or eight persons gathered in Mr. Thorwaldsen's garden. The parties pleaded in person. Mr. Ibsen said that he wanted his net. Mr. Thorwaldsen made short work of him. He pointed out that Mr. Ibsen was trying to eat his cake and have it. Mr. Ibsen was not a bit abashed. He seemed genuinely amused at being caught out like that. His neighbours rallied him unmercifully. In their eyes he had committed the merest peccadillo. Mr. Ibsen replied in kind, and they all laughed gaily. Even Oberhausen and I were infected by their deplorable levity. But Mr. Thorwaldsen put an end to our merriment by stating that the net would be confiscated and Mr. Ibsen would be fined. Mr. Ibsen, with a "don't care" shrug, laughed again most naughtily; he was invincibly cheery. Then Oberhausen's kind heart misgave him. He begged for mercy for Mr. Ibsen. Let the net be taken, but let not an old man be dragged before the magistrate. If he would apologise—Mr. Ibsen clutched at the olive branch, apologised, and said he would not do it again. We were all immensely relieved. One wanted to tell Mr. Ibsen to come out of the corner. The incident closed in a burst of laughter when I handed the sea-trout to Mrs. Thorwaldsen, with a request to let us have it for dinner. We took five more nets in the next fortnight. These people cannot regard poaching seriously.

XXXIX

OF PURFLING AGAIN, WITH A COLLOQUY

THIS afternoon, as I came out of the Island withy-bed and crossed the plank, I was aware of a figure, a little upstream, seated by the backwater, and knew it for Purfling. From his complete immobility it was clear that he was fishing. For the moment he was probably simulating a willow, because there were three of those trees close to him. But I for one was not deceived. His pretence was a failure. He did not look in the least like a willow. But he made a very impressive spectacle. He sat full in the glare of the sinking sun, and a little glory, as of purism, seemed to surround him. Wonder at the man possessed me that here, conscious of no human beholder, he could yet play his part, maintain his principles, be true to himself. For the first time I realised that Purfling was not a poseur, and, as the very last conceivable reason for him vanished, I broke the silence of the golden afternoon with something very like a guffaw. On second thoughts I am compelled to say that it was exactly like a guffaw. In short, it was a guffaw. Purfling never budged. I trusted that he had not heard me,

I approached him on my stomach through the grass, and when abreast of him bade him a cheery good afternoon. His eyes moved slowly till he saw me. "Ah," he said, "it *was* you. Don't come any nearer, please. There is a nice fish here. I've been over him for the last hour." "Feeding?" I asked. "No," he said shortly. "Have you risen him?" I asked, solely to annoy. "No," he said, more shortly. Purfling arouses something hellish in my nature. "What fly have you tried?" I asked. He became even more rigid than before. He was silent. I was ignored. His left shoulder said plainly, "Please, go away." "Put an alder over him," I said, "and have him out." That touched him, for he sighed. I was no longer ignored. I was pitied. I do not mind whether Purfling pities or ignores me, but perhaps his pity is the more complimentary. I lit a cigarette and remained close to Purfling. "Do you mind," I asked in my most servile way, "if I stay and watch you fish. I have never seen you fish, Purfling." Flattery could not reach this man. "Please stay," he said. "You have as much right in this meadow as I." At that moment a motor-horn sounded from the road, and Purfling with astonishing control of his muscles began to subside slowly, slowly into the long grass. I watched him apprehensively. When he had finally come to earth and had begun to crawl from the bank I said, " Purfling, for Heaven's sake ! I'm off this minute." " It's not you," he said graciously, " it's my car. I have a meeting at Little Harmony to-night. Please don't disturb yourself."

The man had watched his fish for an hour, and at the first hoot of his waiting car he left it. This was not human, but it was Purfling. " My dear man," I cried, " try an alder over your fish before you go." He sighed again and went away from me, without a single backward look at the water. It occurred to me that his Christian name must be Talus.

Here was a wretched fish abandoned by Purfling with the utmost callousness. I am not callous. I assumed Purfling's responsibilities on the instant. I got up and looked over the rushes that fringed the bank.

Eighteen yards away in a rippling shallow lay the large trout which I had expected to see. It was moving its tail very gently. It lay in the shade of a willow branch. It was an excessively easy cast.

I began to throw an alder towards it, and at the

ninth cast this fly lit not far away from the fish's head.

The fish took the fly confidingly into its mouth.

Shortly afterwards I hit the fish on the head and placed it in my basket.

A motor-horn sounded. I looked towards the road. Purfling in his car was trying not to run over a flock of sheep.

Now read this. I call it

ISAAC ON A CHALK STREAM

(Piscator, Venator, Raptor,[1] Corydon)

Pisc: Well met, my loving scholar. You have prevented me, I see.

Ven : Ay, marry, good master. I have awaited your coming this hour. Shall we be walking towards the river ?

Pisc: Nay, sir, you have been betimes indeed. But there is no cause to be so brisk. Trust me, on such a dull day we shall find no fly on the water thus early. And it is my purpose to drink my morning's draught in this same good ale-house where you have so patiently expected me. Hostess, a cup of your best drink. Another. Come, I will try a third.

---

[1] In English, Pot-hunter.

VEN: But, sir, were it not· better to be by the water-side? There is no chance of a fish here.

PISC: As much, my honest scholar, as beside the very stream. The fly will not show before seven minutes after eleven of the clock, at soonest. Hostess, a draught of ale.

VEN: Good Master, you do amaze me. How know you this so surely?

PISC: Let me tell you, sir, that your fly is a creature very obedient to the action of the elements. On a grey morning, such as we have to-day, he lacketh the genial warmth of the sun to bring him forth. But forth he must come, will he, nill he, and that he will do this morning at seven after eleven. Nor will he fail us. Come, will you drink a civil glass with me?

VEN: Most gladly, sir; but I had rather be a-fishing. See, the sun is shining now.

PISC: Fear not, worthy scholar; the fly will appear neither sooner nor later than I say.

VEN: I pray you, master, tell me how you have got this prodigious knowledge?

PISC: Marry, sir, by learning. But I confess that no direction can be given to make weather-wise a man of dull capacity. Your good health, my impatient scholar.

Ven: But, sir, may we not take some trouts, though there be no fly?

Pisc: Scholar, you are young to the angle, and so you stand excused. This is the talk of your pot-hunting fishers who do not scruple to throw an alder to a trout that is breakfasting on green drakes. Let me tell you, scholar, that no honest angler will wet a line until the fly be up. Hostess, a pot of ale.

Ven: Good master, I crave your pardon. Shall we not be going?

Pisc: Why, my honest scholar, I think we shall, for it is now eleven of the clock, and it is no more than seven minutes' walk to Willows Bridge, where I do purpose to begin.

.   .   .   .   .   .

Ven: Sir, there is a gentleman on the bridge.

Pisc: An angler, by his rod; and, by his reaching the river at this hour, one who hath skill in the craft. Good-day, sir.

Rapt: Good-morrow, sir. What sport?

Pisc: Why, sir, none.

Rapt: None, sir? You have been fishing to ill purpose then.

Pisc: Nay, sir, I have been fishing to no ill purpose, for I have not been fishing at all.

Rapt: Then, sir, you have my sympathy, for a merrier hour's work I have never known. I have taken the number limit, three brace of as fine trouts as ever were seen. There is eighteen pounds weight here, in my fish-bag.

Ven: This is some pot-hunting fisherman, I fear.

Pisc: Why, sir, you have indeed been fortunate. But I am told that a silver doctor, run through these Clere hatch-holes——

Rapt: A murrain o' your silver doctors, sir! It was a dark olive quill.

Pisc: Indeed, sir?

Rapt: Ay, marry! The rise of a lifetime, sir. The fly came on at nine of the clock, but there hath been none for this half-hour, and so I am for home with my three brace.

Pisc: To sell them at the fishmonger's, sir?

Rapt: Good-day, sir.

Ven: Alas, I fear we have lost some noble sport.

Pisc: I fear that this good gentleman is a liar. Did you mark, scholar, how he made no offer to show us this great catch of trouts?

Ven: True, good master. Then we are to doubt his story?

Pisc: Most shrewdly.

VEN: I see no fly, and it is eight minutes past the hour.

PISC: Nay, my most particular scholar, would you hold me to a minute? No man may be so nice as to the moment of its coming. We shall see it in good time, never fear. Hand me your rod; a pretty tool indeed, but ill-balanced and something too limber for our manner of fishing. See, this is mine; stiff, springy, and lovable. I use no other. With this rod, no matter how bloweth the wind, I will lay my fly on a sixpence at twenty-five yards in the first throw. It is to yours, scholar, as the day is to the night.

VEN: Indeed, master, I have so little of the art that I can find no difference between them. The tackle-maker hath served me ill, for he sold me this same rod as a perfect copy of your own.

PISC: These tackle-makers are for the most part arrant knaves. But, scholar, I see that you have already tied on your fly; and a detached badger— a most unworthy contrivance. Trust me, this is not what honest fishermen are used to do.

VEN: Nay, master, never scold me; I did but wish to be ready.

PISC: Trust me, you do but waste your time; for while it hath been computed that there are no less than seven thousand six hundred and forty-three different sorts of fly tied by these same

T

scoundrelly tackle-merchants, there can be but one or two natural kinds of insects on the river's surface. Thus, scholar, it is in the neighbourhood of four thousand to one that when the fly comes (and it is a plaguy long time a-coming) you must take off this lure and put up another.

VEN: Well, sir, I have a goodly store. See how many sorts are in this pretty box of mine, each in its separate compartment. Is there not a brave show here?

PISC: A brave show, I warrant you. Oh, my poor scholar! How many hath the villain sold you? One, two—twelve! Trust me, scholar, no honest fisherman needs more than three.

VEN: Then have I been tricked most vilely. Tell me, sir, what are these three patterns of which you speak?

PISC: The olive quill, light and dark, and the Piscator's Fancy, so called because your unworthy master devised it. See, it is a little similar to the Wickham, but with this essential difference: the silk is turned around the hook to the right instead of to the left. With these three flies I will catch trouts at any time, I'll hold you two to one, nor will I ask for any other pattern.

VEN: See, master, there is a great trout.

PISC: Where? Where?

VEN : There, good master—a most lovel fish.

PISC : Scholar, you must get you sharper eyes. Do you not see it is a bit of weed ?

VEN : But look, dear master. There—it riseth.

PISC : Lend me your rod. I have no fly tied on.

VEN : Nay, master, you know that I have a detached badger. Would you use such a lure ?

PISC : Why, scholar, it will prove merry sport to take him so. Come, your rod ; I warrant you I will fit you with a trout for supper. Note, scholar, how I shall lay my fly three inches above his nose. A plague take the wind !

VEN : Methought five yards too much on this side.

PISC : Nay, this was but a trial cast. So, I have got his length. There—that was another trial. No man may fish in such a gale with such a rod.

VEN : Good master, do you take your own, and while you tie on a fly let me angle for this trout.

PISC : Prithee, fair scholar, cut me off this willow branch that I may regain my hook. Come, we must try other measures with this gentleman. My Fancy shall go forth in quest of him. Scholar, I must again crave your aid ; it is somewhere in the small of my jacket.

VEN : Now, sir, you are fancy free. I pray you, let me have my rod.

Pisc These olives will not tempt him. He is a dainty fellow. See with what scorn he regardeth the pink Wickham; and the ginger quill fareth no better than the sherry spinner, nor the Welshman's button, neither. We must e'en put up a red caterpillar. No? Then an orange tag.

Ven: Now, sir, I have given you all my patterns.

Pisc: The fiend run away with this fish! Have you any salmon flies about you?

Ven: Nay, sweet master.

Pisc: Then do you essay to catch him. Is a foe worthy of your steel.

Ven: Thank you, sir. I will try this same detached badger once again. See, master, I have him.

Pisc: Well done, scholar. Keep up your point or all is lost. Reel in your line, scholar—give him line. Oh me! These weeds must be your undoing, I fear. Bravely, scholar, bravely! Give him line— reel in—he is a prodigious stout fish. Shall I take the rod?

Ven: No.

Pisc: Well, you have bungled through, scholar, and now he is your own. Well done, sir! A pound if he is an ounce, and were a good fish an he were in season; but I do find him something lean and lousy and unwholesome. Shall we not throw him in again and let him grow till he is more worthy of your anger ?

VEN : Nay, sir, my scales make two pounds and one quarter, and I do think him to be a vastly fine trout. There—he is dead.

PISC : See, sir, there is some fly coming down, as I said it would.

VEN : Then, master, we may look for more sport, I trust, for I do protest that I am quite in love with this fishing. My dear master, what are you doing ?

PISC : Marry, scholar, I am catching one of these same flies, for let me tell you that unless your lure is to the shadow of a shade the same as the fly that these trouts are taking, you shall labour to more purpose in yonder three-acre pasture.

VEN : Well, good master, I will e'en try my detached badger over yonder trout that I see busy by the willow.

PISC : You will not take him. Here cometh a fly, close in, if I can but reach him. Zounds ! I am in to the waist.

VEN : Give me your hand, dear master. Nay, sir, you are woefully stuck.

PISC : . . . .

VEN: Here is help. Good fellow, lend me your aid.

COR: Marnin', gentlemen both. Lar, naow, if it bean't Measter Piscator. Zure as my name be Corydon, 'tis. Swimmin', be 'ee, zur? Cayn't catch these-air trouts thataway, zur. Haw! Haw!

PISC: . . . .

VEN: Nay, good master, this honest man meaneth well by us. Prithee, brave Corydon.

COR: Naow, zur—one, two, three—and up comes the——

PISC: Donkey!

COR: If you please, zur.

PISC: I am soundly drenched. Corydon, are you not keeper here, and is not that your cottage?

COR: Ay, zur.

PISC: Then, friend, you shall fit me with a dry pair of breeches. Scholar, I will presently return.

VEN: And while you are gone, I will match my poor skill against yonder lusty fish.

PISC: Nay, scholar, he is too far for you, trust me. Leave him, and on my return I shall show you a pretty piece of angling. Make your way below bridge where I do see some tidy trouts busy, who are more within your capacity. Come, good Corydon.

.   .   .   .   .   .

VEN: Nay, I will angle for these sprats no longer; there is no hooking them. I will e'en go try for the big fellow, for I do believe that I can reach him. Ay, he is still at work. Marry, by his rise he is a trout indeed. So, another cast and I cover him.

PISC: Why, most naughty scholar, do I find you so heedless of my counsels?

VEN: My loving master, are you back already?

PISC: Ay, our worthy keeper, Corydon, hath furnished me out with these coarse, rough small-clothes. I would they fitted me less straitly, but beggars may not be choosers, eh, honest Corydon?

COR: Why, zur, there wasn' no more'n they two pay-er fer 'ee to chuse amongst; but 'ee did zurely chuse the best.

PISC: There is a penny for you.

COR: Thank 'ee, zur.

PISC: Spend it wisely; let us not find you be-mused with liquor this evening, when we come to leave the water. And now we do not need an attendant, so go your ways, for I mean to catch yonder trout for this gentleman's supper. Come, scholar, give place, and you shall soon see him at closer quarters.

VEN: Dear master, I have but this moment got his length.

Pisc: Nay, sir, you cannot take him; you have not the skill to throw so far; you will surely crack off your fly. Catch me one of these trouts below this bridge, them that I told you of.

Ven: Oh, sir, they are little things.

Cor: They be daäce, zur.

Pisc: Go your ways, Corydon; I tell you that they are trouts. Well, scholar, perhaps you will be better employed watching me. Why, it is a long cast, beshrew me! How now? My fly is gone! Mark this, scholar, and learn how the best may be caught napping. The gut hath been overlong drying and hath broken. Now, I am ready again. There—I think that was pretty well.

Ven: Your fly is in the tree, sir.

Pisc: Ah, scholar, this time your eyes have not deceived you; it is as you say. Oh me! I am most evilly hung up. Now, while I am mending the damage, let me tell you, sir, that when I shall hook yonder fish I must manage him yarely. Do you see these beds of green weeds? He will surely run for them, and once among them, he is lost to us, but you shall see how I shall master him.

Ven: That was a fine cast, sir. Oh, he hath taken it.

Pisc: Ay, hath he, and he is mine own.

VEN: Have a care, sir; he is for the weeds.

PISC: . . . .

VEN: Oh, sir. What is to be done now?

PISC: Marry, a strong fish; no man alive could have held him; but I have not done with him, scholar. Mark now, how I shall play him with the hand. See, a gentle pull and draw; a steady sawing motion of the arm, and——

COR: Haw! Haw!

PISC: Corydon, we do not desire your company. Come, scholar, let us be going, for there is a notable pool beyond this meadow where I have seen as many as twenty valiant trouts feeding at a time. And when we are come to this pool we will sit beneath one of those tall elms and rest from our toil awhile. For let me tell you that the sun is now so hot and high that it is odds against our seeing anything to repay our casting. But there we will take our dinner pleasantly, feasting blamelessly among the buttercups like these same silly kine; and I will give you yet more directions, for I would fain make you an artist.

VEN: Well, sir, I will confess that a sandwich will not come amiss.

PISC: Nay, scholar, an your stomach be for sandwiches I must pity you; for let me tell you, sir, that I do abhor your sandwiches. A greasy,

soft, and flimsy food, more fitted for the tea-table
of a gentlewoman than for the dinner of an honest
angler. It is ever my way to carry with me in
my fish-bag a cold pullet's leg and a lettuce, a
piece of good, dry wheaten bread, and such fruit
as is in season. Ah hah! sir, I see your mouth
begin to water. What say you to the providence
of an old angler? Come, scholar, here is our tree,
and now let us fall to.

VEN: Oh, master, what is the matter?

PISC: That feather-brained wench hath forgotten
to furnish me with my dinner. A murrain——

VEN: Nay, my loving master, will you not
share mine? A sandwich——

PISC: Oh, my dear scholar, shall I not be rob-
bing you? Thank you, sir, I will try another. I
protest that these sandwiches are vastly well;
though this one hath more gristle in it than I could
wish. Nay, sir, but one more and I am filled.
No more, I thank you.

VEN: Why, sir, I shall not eat it; would you
see it wasted?

PISC: Nay, that were a sin, and I would rather
have it on my stomach than on my conscience.

VEN: You are merry, sir.

PISC: That is a gallant hunch of cake.

VEN: Will you try it, sir?

Pisc: Very gladly, scholar. What goodly plums are here! Oh me! your cake hath stones in it, sir. Whither now, good scholar?

Ven: A fish rose, sir.

Pisc: Can you point him out?

Ven: Nay, sir, I have my eye upon the very spot in the middle of the pool, but I should be hard put to it to show it to you. Why, I have him at the first attempt.

Pisc: I will put the net under him for you, for let me tell you, scholar, that this feat is no easy one, and not to be essayed by an unskilful hand. For if in landing of a fish the net do but touch the line, he shall break all. Bring him nearer to this tussock—so——

Ven: Alas, master, he is gone.

Pisc: Scholar, you will do better yet, but I must tell you that you managed clumsily. Why did you suffer the line to touch the net?

Ven: Dear master, it seemed to me——

Pisc: No matter, sir. You will do better, trust me. I have in you a towardly scholar, but no one may learn this art in a morning's fishing. I protest that the day is over sultry; I will sit awhile beneath this fine tree and read old Epictetus in the shade. Angle, if you will; but, trust me, you may not look for sport before evening.

V<small>EN</small>: Up, dear master, the trouts are rising madly.

P<small>ISC</small>: My shaving-water, Thomas.

V<small>EN</small>: Nay, sweet master, awake. It is six of the clock, and there is great sport toward.

P<small>ISC</small>: As I live, I do believe that I have nodded. Ay, scholar, the trouts are rising gallantly. Let me tell you that this is the evening rise, called amongst us old anglers Tom Fool's Light, because it would seem that the veriest bungler must enjoy sport when the fish are so ready to feed. But you must know, sir, that this name is ill-chosen. For all their boldness it taketh a master hand to deceive them at this time.

V<small>EN</small>: Yet have I landed a leash in this very pool.

P<small>ISC</small>: Then I will go higher yet, and try conclusions with them in the next meadow.

.   .   .   .   .   .

V<small>EN</small>: Well, master, the sun hath set upon a fair day and a happy one for me. I have taken another brace since we parted company. How hath fortune smiled upon you, good master, beside this tumbling bay?

P<small>ISC</small>: Why, sir, sourly, for I have wasted all this fine rise fishing for one trout, which, when

I had caught him, proved too small for keeping. So I gave him his liberty.

VEN : Why, sir, what fly is this? Here is a woundily big hook, and here is a brave show of silver tinsel and peacock herl.

PISC : It is a sedge-fly that came by accident among my tackle.

VEN : Here comes friend Corydon, the keeper, to lead you to your dry clothes.

PISC : Prithee, sweet scholar, not a word about the sedge-fly. Our day is ended, and I am glad to see that you have profited so well by my instruction.

VEN : And by your example, fair master.

XL

OF DEATH

I AM sitting beside the Island Pool where the river pauses for a moment to circle solemnly round, then flows on its way in a broad green and amber glide. The Island Pool is deep and dark and mysterious. Immortal fishes of incredible size sometimes swim into the ken of him who, lying flat with his nose over the camp-sheathing, peers into its profundities. But they never rise to the fly.

No fishes in this river ever rise to the fly. They used to, but that is long, long ago—a whole week. And they will never do it again. There is no fly for them to rise to, and if there were they would not rise to it. But there will never be any more fly on this river. Nobody will ever catch a fish here again—on the fly. Dynamite would cause some of them to float belly up. There is something to be said for dynamite after all. Here is an unworthy thought. I would not really use dynamite if I had any. I do not know how to use it. And it might blow my hand off. And how should I fish then?

I do not know that I want to fish any more. As one grows older one gets a new way of looking at things. Youth has a distorted vision. For Turkish Delight at one time I would have bartered my soul. To-day it nauseates me. So with angling. Years ago I would, if I could, have killed trout all day, and under any weight of them staggered home rejoicing; the greater the weight, the louder my rejoicing. In those days my joy was clouded by no misgivings; no compunction dulled my appetite for slaughter. I was wholly callous to any destruction I had wrought. Those bright, dead bodies loaded my back only. My soul——did I have a soul then? Who knows? But had I succeeded in bartering it for Turkish Delight, the other party to the transaction would infallibly have been swindled— however little of his wares he had yielded. Yes, I gloried in butchery.

And to-day? Well, lately I have had doubts. They have always been put sternly away, for the angling habit strikes deep roots, and it is foolish to examine settled convictions. Only misery can come of it. And, until the last year or two, my conviction that trout exist for anglers to catch has been founded on the rock. But now I find that it needs shoring up a little. I dwell more and more on (yet get less and less satisfaction out of) the Dominion of Man, his supreme place in the creation, his right to dispose of the lives of inferior creatures. I am not content to kill; I must justify the killing. I find man—myself—slaying right and left, and I cry out that his title to do so is unquestionable—thereby questioning it. And is the argument sufficient? Is there not something like an ignoratio elenchi here? (If one were only certain what an ignoratio elenchi is.)

Again, by constantly telling myself and other people that it is so, I nearly always succeed in believing firmly that cold-blooded animals have not the same power of sensation as warm-blooded animals—that fish, for example, do not feel pain, being provided (trout, at any rate) with horny mouths whose substance is comparable to the human nail, and—it does not hurt to cut one's nails—therefore unsensitive to the penetration of a hook. At one time I have even persuaded myself to look on this circumstance as a direct proof of the Creator's intentions regarding trout and men. But there are other fishes that have soft mouths— roach, for example. Thank goodness I have few roach on my conscience.

Once more—how very much better it is for a wild animal to die at the hand of man than, after a miserable and wasting old age, of starvation. For this is the undoubted end of all such creatures as escape destruction at the fangs of their fellows. Thus we defend fox-hunting, thus hare-coursing, thus the pheasant battue. At first sight the argument seems unanswerable. It is certainly best to die quickly. But to live long—that, too, is good. There, I feel, is a sort of point of view. I know it is a foolish one, but it sticks in my mind.

Away from the river I can see the force of all these observations. But on the bank they have less force. Perhaps I put my head carefully over a bank, and there, not six feet below my eyes, is a trout, a great golden-green fellow in the prime of his splendid life. Three pounds he weighs (when I grass him). He has won gallantly through the perils of his fishing days, swimming faster, exercising more wariness, feeding harder than the others of his year. And now, one out of—what is it, a hundred thousand?—two hundred million? —that have succumbed, he lies there in the sunlight just above cool emerald weeds, sucking in the sweet little duns as his bountiful stream carries them above his head. With what ease he keeps his place against the rapid current; with what whole-hearted, admirable gluttonry he gulps his breakfast; what a gorgeous, lithe, perfect animal is this that I would strike into hideous rigidity.

U

The heart is black that can plot mischief to this excellent creature. How many years of joyous dun-devouring life are before him? Five—ten—twenty? I see him, a portly ten-pounder, living for ever, for ever stemming this crystal stream with fins that grow broader and stronger, the intoxicating gold and green, vermilion, brown, and blue of his scales growing deeper, richer, more and more splendid. "No," says Argument, "not for ever. And—ultimately? An old, lean, blind, diseased fish, dying by inches. Have him out?" And I have him out.

But while I am doing it, should I work him into still water, can I, while he swims slowly round and round, always in sight, wholly persuade myself that he feels no pain. I grant his horny mouth. But is fear no pain? And does this fish feel no fear? Fear glares from his eyes. He is stricken with it. And against fear he fights, as well as against gut and split cane. I have given this fish seven minutes of utter terror. It is not a comforting thought. I put it away from me.

And now he is in the net. Now he lies at my feet, staring a dull, foolish reproach at me. At this point I have to be very quick if I mean to take that trout home with me. He lies in my hand, passive, dignified, demeaning himself by no futile wriggles. He owns the Lord of Creation. Whang!

The net has done its regal work. A shudder passes through him, through my hand, my arm, to my heart. I have, then, done God's work, which He appointed me to do. This reflection is much more comforting than my last. I hug it to my bosom. I basket the fish. But I am not entirely happy, Ten years ago I should have run all the way home to exhibit my three-pounder. Youth is not to be touched by these morbid thoughts. Happy youth ! The Lord of Creation goes his way with a heavier—basket.

Sometimes, at such moments, a grisly idea has come my way. It seems to me that somewhere there is an Angler who casts baits for men and women. Like these same trout that live and feed and fight and love in their stream, and know nothing of that world of the outer air with its fields and trees and birds and flowers and men, save that vague shadows (some to be feared, others undreadful) move now and then between themselves and the light, so we, in our own element, perfectly satisfied with our three dimensions, and only dimly perceiving the possibility of a fourth, live and feed, love, fight, and amuse ourselves, our equanimity disturbed only by one dreadful shadow which moves at times within our field of vision. What it is we do not know, but it passes, and one of our number is gone. Where we do not know either. But that our turn

will come we know very well. Like these same
trout, we realise a danger, continually imminent,
that lurks in those things we love. But loving them,
feeling the need of them, we pursue them, some
carefully, others recklessly. This danger that we
call death (who knows what that Angler calls it?)
may be hidden anywhere—in an oyster, a hunter,
a footstep cut in eternal ice, a glass of ruby wine,
an open window. Sooner or later, the Angler will
get us. But we avoid his snares as long as we can.
And while our lips proclaim ourselves the Lords of
Creation, our hearts tremble at the presumption.
For we know that it is a lie.

So I think that I shall give up——

.   .   .   .   .   .

Excuse me. A large fish has just risen under
the willow. And here come the duns.

XLI

OF A LARGEST TROUT

THIS evening I took a trout of three and a half pounds. I do not boast about it. It is nothing super-troutish. But it is the largest brown trout I have ever had. It is so obviously the largest that I have ever had, that I have not only weighed it on my own spring, but also on the kitchen scales which I know to be accurate. I tremble to think of the weight to which, when I have time, I shall calculate it on the basis of my own spring's verdict. For my present purpose it is enough that it is my largest trout.

I am continually finding resemblances between angling and life. This is not at all surprising. And I take no credit to myself for it. One can (everybody does) draw parallels between life and any pursuit whatever. The only thing that limits one in this direction is one's own speed and endurance in the covering of paper with words or in dictation to the phonograph, supposing one to be an author of sufficient eminence to employ one of those very convenient aids to literature. For as the part possesses many properties of the whole—the finger, for example, of the body, the leaf of the tree, the hay of the haystack, the note of the melody, the drop of the ink, the turf of the lawn, the—I have no phonograph—so, angling being but a part of life, and golf being a part of life, and commerce and wine-bibbing and the adjusting of averages and hanging head downwards from a trapeze with a colleague in one's teeth and studying the Gorilla language and—(really I must get one)—and other things being but parts of life, it follows that the incidents of the greater are reflected in those of the less.

Perhaps I have found the resemblance most marked in this affair of this, my greatest trout. Let me give you a short account of the taking. If you have any humanity at all, you will not deny me this. You need not listen. But I must tell. See, now. There will be a line of dots presently. That will mean that I have done. Then you can tell me about *your* largest trout, and the exact number of yards he ran out, and all the rest of it. That will be much more amusing for you.

It happened in this way.

The place was Crab Hatch. I have hardly ever come to Crab Hatch without finding something

on the move, if it has only been some old horse-
trout minnowing in the glide. On the blankest
days Crab Hatch will offer evidence that the river
is inhabited. It is impossible to be utterly des-
pondent just before reaching Crab Hatch. And
in the late evening it is a solemn and choice spot.
The water circles there eternally, and you never
know what you may get your hook into. A
pounder in that rapid current gives the effect of
the great Leviathan himself, and the reel screeches
and one's heart leaps and the fine strong excitement is yours, yea, though the fish go back. I
cannot allot any but the first place to Crab Hatch.
It is certainly the best spot on the water.

I arrived about eight o'clock.

Ten minutes after I got there I saw a paltry
little rise just on the hump of gravel where the
glide is (and the young graylings are). I cursed it,
because I had hoped to find rising to-night the
Immense Fish which last night rose twice in the
still below the glide. But though I waited his
pleasure for several more seconds, nothing happened to that mirror of the western glory.
Patience, after sunset, does not reside within forty
miles of me. I got out line and threw despon-
dently to the gravel hump a red quill, to be precise,
dressed on a number two or thereabout hook.
Since I was not in luck in the matter of the

Immense Fish, if I put a young grayling down so much the better. My fly fell about ten yards west of the spot at which I had aimed.

Immediately I was playing something of quite respectable strength. It jagged downwards, and I said to my heart; "A grayling of dimensions!" It proceeded down stream, jagging always, and I never saw it until I had followed it fifty yards. Then it showed—yellow. I thought, "The gut is frayed," and stepped up to my middle in water disguised as mud. Subsequently I found myself still connected with the fish. Ten hours (was it?) later I performed a sort of tilting at the ring with trout and landing net (my miserable little landing net) and grassed him. Then (after butchery), while my spring balance, groaning, sank to three, my soul rose towards the zenith. I had topped three pounds. The years fell away from my shoulders.

.   .   .   .   .   .

Thus the great prize came to me, through no special skill or care or pertinacity of mine. It is impossible to draw any moral from the incident which is not quite immoral. I cannot say, "Behold what comes of sticking to it," or "Thus, young man, by perfecting oneself in the use of one's weapons, when the opportunity arises one is found ready to seize it," because I threw without any dogged purpose to achieve, but rather with the peevish object of annoying a small fish which I did not at all wish to catch.   Also, I threw infamously. Also, I ought to have lost my trout, not once, but several times, while playing it.   Also, I was extremely pleased when I had landed it.   I can only say, " Observe the resemblance between this affair and that business of life in which we are all engaged.   To the undeserving the good things go.   Industry is in most cases its own reward.   A complete abstention from toiling and spinning plus a raiment that outshines Solomon are the marks of others than field lilies.   The wicked flourish and die in their beds.   How is one, in short, to account for the undeserving rich upon the accepted principles of morality?"   One can't.   It is simpler to account for the accepted principles of morality as being the invention of the undeserving rich.   If it were so, there is genius in it.

.   .   .   .   .   .

My grandfather died worth a lot of money. Why?   Because he took a sporting chance and it came off.   Had he not done this I should now be competing for a sandwich-board with my betters. Granted that my grandfather deserved his luck, granted that his application to his business of selling bars of iron made him fit to understand the

U 2

possibilities that lay in his sporting chance. But what about me? I have a competence; I eat three square meals a day; I wear warm, if slovenly clothes; I go about at my pleasure; I sit in the dress circle; I travel second-class; I subscribe to Boots; I smoke the best tobacco; I fish in chalk streams; I possess Rose Doré at three shillings a tube; I live like a lord whose estate is not too seriously encumbered. And for the first thirty years of my life I did not begin to pay expenses. I have been the death of many thousands of pounds and I have not earned enough, if spread over the whole of my life, to keep me from starving. In a word I am one of the undeserving rich.

Old Bunting is seventy-five. He rises at four in the morning and goes to bed at nine in the evening. Between those hours he rests perhaps for four. He can make hay, he can hedge and ditch, he can plough and sow and reap and mow, and be a farmer's septuagenarian. He has raised a large family of strong admirable citizens. He lives on bread and tea and beer and cabbage and bacon and a little tinned salmon and a little beef. He smokes something called Coolie Cut. The price of my reel is a week's living to Old Bunting.

And he is contented, nay, happy; delights in hedging; mows with gratitude.

Why, in the name of Injustice? Why?

A long time ago one of the undeserving rich, a person like myself, must have been faced with the same difficulty. Looking upon the ancestor of Old Bunting he must have reflected thus: " In a short time the fellow will notice something and will then proceed to take all my property away from me and hand over to me his in exchange, reserving only for himself that large and exceedingly sharp scythe." Being, unlike myself, a man of extraordinary cleverness, he must have gone to Old Bunting's ancestor, and told him that Industry was the source of Happiness. Old Bunting's ancestor, knowing himself to be excellently industrious, must have been pleased, and never having had time to think for himself, must have accepted the statement on the word of the well-dressed gentleman. Once incorporated with the mental equipment of Old Bunting's ancestor the thing would be handed down through the Bunting generations until it has reached Bunting, our contemporary.

That might account for it.

It is certainly inconceivable that the idea could have originated among the deserving poor.

I have said that I was extremely pleased when I landed my greatest trout.

I am also extremely pleased that I am one of the undeserving rich.

But I am also sorry that there should be so many deserving poor. (What the deuce is it they deserve ?)

And I am also sorry that there should be so many little graylings in the river. But it is so.

XLII

OF DEPARTURE

TO-MORROW we go away.
In half an hour it will be too dark to fish·
Let us hurry on to the Mill pool. I always
hurry on to the Mill pool, for it used to be the best
place on the river. Here is broad water and deep,
scooping out the bank in a great S all along which
the little dimpling rises were wont long ago to tell
of great feeding trouts. I always hope to see
them again.

Perhaps to-night.

Below the Mill hatch is camp sheathing, thirty
yards of it and rough water against it. And you
know what that means. Only this summer it
doesn't. Below the camp sheathing is a willow.
Its roots, in the rough water, always hold a patch
of floating weed, and you know what that ought
to mean.

Below this willow is a thin rapid which is never
without its rises (but they are all little graylings
this year). And out on the glide beyond there was

formerly always a tidy trout. And in under the
alder bush below there may be anything up to
five pounds. But there won't be.

Oh! the Mill pool used to be a great institution.

It is a great institution. For I will lash my
poor old Hope yet again into activity. To-morrow
I shall have no further use for her. For to-morrow
we go away.

The Mill pool is a great institution. I declare
it. I profess it. It is placed on the top of the
water, which is the right situation for a Mill pool.
It never fails. I say it never fails. It will not
fail me to-night. It is inconceivable that the
Mill pool should ever fail.

What though the Lower End lie dead and dull
at ten o'clock? What though at midday the long
withy-bed yield nothing but broken gut and filled
waders? What though, by two, the Island has
beaten a man, and the backwater above it by four,
and the Slow Water by five, and the Bridge Reach
by six, and Crab Hatch by seven, and the Crab backwater by eight, and the Two Meadows by nine.
Hurry on to the Mill. A red sedge will do the
trick yet. There is half an hour more of light,
and the pool is in the very eye of the afterglow.

Nothing is rising in the Mill pool.

And to-morrow we go away.

.   .   .   .   .   .

The end of our time here has approached with frightful rapidity. For the last week I have been going about a prey to settled gloom. Every passing second has seemed to bring me a day nearer to exile. I have not fished. I have rested upon my three-and-a-half pounder. No anti-climaxes for me.

What am I doing with this rod and landing net, by the Mill pool?

Oh, my dear sir, I am not a consistent person at all, you know. Besides, I am not really fishing. Only saying good-bye. And it is madness to come near a river without a rod.

Besides, look at the water. Look at it, I say. What chance do you fancy I have of an anti-climax? I said there were to be none for me.

.   .   .   .   .   .

To-morrow we go away.

The thoughts of that very large fish has done a little—only a little—to check the galloping of the moments.

It is matter for speculation at what moment in a season of bliss the character of time's flight changes. Two months ago I remember the end of every day was celebrated by me with slappings on the back because I had by so much increased the sum of my enjoyment of Willows. I counted the hours I had had.

For a long time, now, I have counted those that remain.

When did I change my attitude towards time's advance ? I do not know, but I know that to-day I regard its haste with despair.

Touching that much longer, more varied and even more delightful sojourn upon which I am engaged I have not, I fancy, yet reached the dividing point. Still (more than ever in the past two years), I hug the possession of my days as they are completed; not yet do I regard them as gone. Still I reach out to meet them as they come, welcoming them as good full friends, not frowning upon them as evanescent tricksters who dawn but to close. I hope to be doing the same when (and if) I am a hundred and forty. I can never see why that fellow Death should be permitted to spoil one's time here. Let him be content with his certain win or wins (for he commonly gets in more than one shrewd knock at a man). Physically, I admit him my superior, because I have to. I am not his match at all. I own it.

(A lot he cares.) But I decline to have him blundering about in front of me when I am painting, or throwing stones in the water when I am fishing, or sitting third with my wife and me. And I laugh at him. For I know that in whatever I do, I am achieving immortality—even when I write—not the immortality of my miserable name, but the immortality of my doings and words, each least one of which has its influence now and for ever. As the splash of my cocked dun shall be felt in Orion and further and further than that, till Orion ceases to be and afterwards and afterwards, so my lightest good-morning has within it the welfare or misery of men to come. And this is said humbly and not otherwise. Let my good mornings therefore be as good as I can make them and my good nights and all that lies between.

But though I dismiss from my consideration the General Terminator of Pleasant Experiences, I cannot look with equal contempt upon the day of my departure from this place. The first is an uncertain certainty, incalculable, foolishness to brood upon.

But the boxes are packed.

And now it is too dark for any more fishing. Let us reel up for the year—Someone is waiting for me. There, above Ottley Down, is the glow of the coming moon, which is to light my wife and me on our last walk round the village.

And as we must be alone for this, I will wish you good-bye.

WILLIAM BRENDON AND SON, LTD.
PRINTERS, PLYMOUTH